SO YOU NEED TO SOURCE A PRODUCT OVERSEAS?

SO YOU NEED TO SOURCE A PRODUCT OVERSEAS?

How to Establish an Efficient and Resilient Supply Chain

JOHN C. RAMIG

FunnelFlow Press

CONTENTS

Printed in the United States of America
First Printing, 2023
Print ISBN - 9798218138943
Case Laminate ISBN - 9798218167561
EPUB ISBN - 9798218138950

FUNNELFLOW PRESS
3137 Tiger Run Court #105
Carlsbad, CA 92010
www.FunnelFlow.io/press

INTRODUCTION: LIFE TAKES UNEXPECTED TURNS

"Two roads diverged in a wood, and I –
I took the one less traveled by,
and that has made all the difference."
—Robert Frost

My background is rooted in politics and law, and up until a few years ago, I was busily building a corporate law practice. Then I made the leap to being an entrepreneur when I got involved in a footwear business. Over the past 26 years, I have earned an advanced degree in international trade, mostly through the school of hard knocks! By last count, I had made over 115 trips to Asia. I also founded a business, served as its CEO, and sold it in China. The purpose of this book is to share some of what I have learned, and I hope these lessons will help you along the way.

Through good times and bad, international trade continues to grow because it is good business. Manufacturing outsourcing raises profit margins, improves inventory management, and gets new products to the market faster. It also improves product quality and customer service levels. Manufacturing outsourcing allows you to utilize assets that others already have in place, without having to make a heavy investment developing your own capabilities. This frees capital to grow your business. Manufacturing outsourcing also provides access to third party design, manufacturing expertise, and the flexibility to scale production up or down quickly.

But if COVID-19-related disruptions have taught us anything, it's that a business needs to be smart when setting up its supply chain, and, once the supply chain is established, it should be constantly monitored in order to adjust and respond to the ever-changing circumstances.

Outsourcing the manufacturing of your product requires a skillset unfamiliar to most small businesses. It requires the understanding of foreign business culture, multilingual communications, and an approach to business that is a prudent mixture of trust and verification. Relying on expert advice will save you time, generate cost savings, and enhance the resiliency of your supply chain.

Outsourcing the manufacturing of your product also requires a willingness to invest in cross-cultural relationships by treating your suppliers with consideration and respect. Successful supply chains are based on the mutual benefit of each link in the chain. Therefore, careful attention to nurturing each link is critical to success.

Over the years, I've had the privilege to bear witness to the economic miracle of international trade. It provides the opportunity to improve the lives of people by creating jobs and brings superior quality products to market faster and at lower cost. It is without question one of the world's best anti-poverty programs. And so long as the rules of international trade are both fair and enforced in order to protect workers and the environment, the benefits of growing international trade are compelling.

We live in a global economy. Businesses must be nimble and have a global perspective to stay competitive. It's been my privilege over the past 26 years to help businesses develop successful supply chains, mitigate the inherent trade risks associated with international trade, and succeed in the global economy.

I hope this book helps you better understand what is necessary to establish an efficient and resilient supply chain—because your business may depend on it.

| 1 |

A SELECTED HISTORY OF GLOBAL TRADE – AND WHY IT KEEPS GROWING[1]

"Every man lives by exchanging." —Adam Smith

The trade of goods and services is as old as humankind. From the time when simple bartering began, people have been trading goods. The purpose of including a brief history of global trade in this book, and its economic rationale, is simple. As stated by a great prophet, "There is nothing new under the sun!" If you understand your outsourcing project in a broader historical context, your likelihood of success is increased.

Silk Road

As of the first century B.C., a remarkable phenomenon started. For the first time in history, luxury products from China started to appear at the other edge of the Eurasian continent—in Rome. They got there after being hauled for thousands of miles along the Silk Road. With the Silk Road, trade had stopped being a local or regional affair and started to become global.

This is not to say globalization had started in earnest. Silk was mostly a luxury good, and so were the spices that were added to the intercontinental trade between Asia and Europe. As a percentage of the total economy, the value of these exports was tiny, and many middlemen were involved to get the goods to their destination. But global trade links were established, and for those involved, it was a goldmine. From purchase price to final sale price, the multiple went in the dozens. The Silk Road could prosper in part because two great empires dominated much of the route. If trade was interrupted, it was often because of blockades by local enemies of China or Rome.

When the Silk Road eventually closed, as it did after several centuries, the fall of the empire had everything to do with it. And when it reopened in Marco Polo's late medieval time, it was because of the rise of a hegemonic empire: the Mongols. This is a pattern we will see throughout the history of trade: it thrives when nations protect it, and it fails when they don't.

Spice Route

The next chapter in trade happened thanks to the Islamic merchants. As the new religion spread in all directions from its original Arabian heartland in the seventh century, so did trade. The founder of Islam, the prophet Mohammed, was a famous merchant, as was his wife, Khadija. Trade was thus in the DNA of the new religion and its followers, and that showed. By the early ninth century, Muslim traders had already dominated in Mediterranean and Indian Ocean trade. Afterwards, they could be found in as far as Indonesia. But the main focus of Islamic trade and the Middle Ages were spices. Unlike silk, spices were mainly traded by sea since ancient times. But by the medieval era, they had become the true focus of international trade. Chief among them were cloves, nutmeg, and mace from the fabled Spice Islands. They were extremely expensive and in demand, also in Europe. But as with silk, they remained a luxury product, and trade remained relatively low volume. Globalization still hadn't really taken off.

The First Wave of Globalization (19th century–1914) – Age of Discovery

Truly global trade kicked off in the age of discovery. It was in this era, from the end of the 15th century though the 18th century that European explorers connected East and West and accidentally discovered the Americas. The age of discovery rocked the world. The most (in)famous "discovery" is that of America by Columbus, which all but ended the pre-Columbian civilizations. But the most consequential exploration, the circumnavigation of Magellan, had opened the door to the Spice Islands, cutting out Arab and Italian middlemen. While trade once again remained small compared to the total size of the overall worldwide economy, it certainly altered people's lives. Potatoes, tomatoes, coffee, and cocoa were introduced in Europe, and the price of spices fell steeply. Still economists today don't regard this era as one of true globalization. Trade certainly started and became global, and it had even been the main reason for starting the Age of Discovery. But the resulting global economy was still very much siloed and lopsided. The European empire set of global supply chains, but mostly with those colonies they owned. Moreover, their colonial model was chiefly one of exploitation, including the shameful legacy of the slave trade. Empires thus created both a mercantilist and colonial economy, but not a truly globalized one.

The first wave of globalization began early in the 19th century and continued until World War I. By the end of the 18th century, Great Britain had started to dominate the world both geographically, through the establishment of the British Empire, and technologically, with innovations like the steam engine, the industrial weaving machine and more. It was the era of the First Industrial Revolution. The "British" Industrial Revolution made for a fantastic twin engine of global trade. On the one hand, steamships and trains could transport goods over thousands of miles, both within countries and across countries. On the other hand, its industrialization allowed Britain to make products that were in demand all over the world, like iron, textiles, and manufactured goods. With its advanced industrial technologies Britain was able to attack a huge and rapidly expanding international market.

The resulting globalization was obvious in the numbers. For about a century, trade grew on average 3% per year. That growth rate propelled exports from a share of 6% of global GDP in the early 19th century, to 14% on the eve of World War I. As John Maynard Keynes, the economist, observed: "The inhabitant of London could order by telephone, sipping his morning tea in bed, the various products of the whole Earth, in such quantity as he might see fit, and reasonably expect their early delivery upon his doorstep."

And Keynes also noted a similar situation was also true in the world of investing. Those with the means in New York, Paris, London, or Berlin could also invest in internationally active joint stock companies. One of those, the French Compagnie de Suez, constructed the Suez Canal, connecting the Mediterranean with the Indian Ocean and opened yet another artery of world trade. Others built railways in India or managed mines in African colonies. Foreign direct investment, too, was globalizing.

While Britain was the country that benefited most from this globalization, as it had the most capital and technology, others did too, by exporting their goods. The invention of the refrigerated cargo ship or "reefer ship" in the 1870s, for example, allowed for countries like Argentina and Uruguay to enter their golden age. They started to mass export meat, from cattle grown on their vast lands. Other countries, too, started to specialize their production in those fields in which they were most competitive.

But the first wave of globalization and industrialization also coincided with darker events. By the end of the 19th century, most globalizing and industrialized European nations grabbed for a piece of Africa, the only independent country left on the continent was Ethiopia. In a similarly negative vein, large countries like India, China, Mexico, or Japan, which were previously powers to reckon with, were either not able or not allowed to adapt to the industrial and global trends. Either the Western powers put restraints on their independent development or they were otherwise outcompeted because of their lack of access to capital or technology. Finally, many workers in the industrialized nations also did not benefit from globalization—their work commoditized by industrial machinery, or their output undercut by foreign imports.

The World Wars

The outbreak of World War I brought an end to just about everything the burgeoning high society of the West had gotten so used to, including globalization. The ravage was complete. Millions of soldiers died in battle, millions of civilians died as collateral damage, war replaced trade, destruction replaced construction, and countries closed their borders yet again.

In the years between the world wars, the financial markets, which were still connected in a global web, caused a further breakdown of the global economy and its links. The Great Depression in the US led to the end of the economic boom in South America, and a run on the banks in many other parts of the world. Another world war followed in 1939–1945. By the end of World War II, trade as a percentage of world GDP had fallen to 5%, a level not seen in more than a hundred years.

Second and Third Waves of Globalization

The story of globalization, however, was not over. The end of the World War II marked a new beginning for the global economy. Under the leadership of a new hegemon, the United States of America, and aided by the technologies of the Second Industrial Revolution, like the car and the plane, global trade started to rise once again. At first, this happened in two separate tracks, as the Iron Curtain divided the world into two spheres of influence. But as of 1989, when the Iron Curtain fell, globalization became a truly global phenomenon.

In the early decades after World War II, institutions like the European Union and other free trade vehicles championed by the US were responsible for much of the increase in international trade. In the Soviet Union, there was a similar increase in trade, albeit through centralized planning rather than the free market. The effect was profound.

Worldwide, trade once again rose to the levels in 1914. In 1989, export once again counted for 14% of global GDP. It was paired with a steep rise in middle-class incomes in the West.

Then, when the wall dividing East and West fell in Germany, and the Soviet Union collapsed, globalization became an all-conquering force. The newly created World Trade Organization (WTO) encouraged nations all over the world to enter into free-trade agreements, and most of them did, including many newly independent ones. In 2001, even China, which for the better part of the 20th century had been a secluded, agrarian economy, became a member of the WTO, and started to manufacture for the world. In this "new" world, the US set the tone and led the way, but many others benefited in their slipstream.

At the same time, a new technology from the Third Industrial Revolution, the internet, connected people all over the world in an even more direct way. The orders Keynes could place by phone in 1914 could now be placed over the internet. Instead of having them delivered in a few weeks, they would arrive at one's doorstep in a few days. What was more, the internet also allowed for a further global integration of value chains. You could do R&D in one country, sourcing in others, production in yet another, and distribution all over the world.

The result has been a globalization on steroids. In the 2000s, global exports reached a milestone, as they rose to about a quarter of global GDP. Trade, the sum of imports and exports, consequentially grew to about half of the world's GDP. In some countries, like Singapore, Belgium, or others, trade is worth much more than 100% of GDP. A majority of global population has benefited from this: more people than ever before belong to the global middle class and hundreds of millions achieved that status by participating in the global economy.

Globalization Today

That brings us to today, when a new wave of globalization is once again upon us. In a world increasingly dominated by two global powers, the US and China, the new frontier of globalization is the cyber world.

The digital economy, in its infancy during the third wave of globalization, is now becoming a force to reckon with through e-commerce, digital services, and 3D printing. It is further enabled by artificial intelligence but threatened by cross-border hacking and cyberattacks.

At the same time, a negative globalization is expanding too, through the global effect of climate change. Pollution in one part of the world leads to extreme weather events in another. And the cutting of forests in the few "green lungs" the world has left, like the Amazon rainforest, has a further devastating effect on not just the world's biodiversity, but its capacity to cope with hazardous greenhouse gas emissions.

But as this new wave of globalization is reaching our shores, many of the world's people are turning their backs on it. In the West particularly, many middle-class workers are fed up with a political and economic system that has resulted in economic inequality, social instability, and—in some countries—mass immigration, even if it also led to economic growth and cheaper products. Protectionism, trade wars, and immigration stops are once again the order of the day in many countries.

The Evolving Economic Theories of Global Trade

While global trade had been dominated by different nations and characterized by different products over time, the economic rationale for its existence has also evolved.

Mercantilism

An early theory of global trade, which peaked in the 16th and 17th centuries, was known as mercantilism. Mercantilism focused directly upon the welfare of the nation. It insisted that the acquisition of wealth, particularly wealth in the form of gold, was of paramount importance for national policy. Mercantilists took the virtues of gold almost as an article of faith; consequently, they never sought to explain adequately why the pursuit of gold deserved such a high priority in their economic plans.

Mercantilism was based on the conviction that national interests are inevitably in conflict—that one nation can increase its trade only at the expense of other nations. Thus, governments were led to impose price and wage controls, foster national industries, promote exports of finished goods and imports of raw materials, while at the same time limiting the exports of raw materials and the imports of finished goods. The state endeavored to provide its citizens with a monopoly of the resources and trade outlets of its colonies.

The trade policy dictated by mercantilist philosophy was accordingly simple: encourage exports, discourage imports, and take the proceeds of the resulting export surplus in gold. Mercantilists' ideas often were intellectually shallow, and indeed their trade policy might have been little more than a rationalization of the interests of a rising merchant class that wanted wider markets—hence the emphasis on expanding exports—coupled with protection against competition in the form of imported goods.

A typical illustration of the mercantilist spirit is the English Navigation Act of 1651, which reserved for the home country the right to trade with its colonies and prohibited the import of goods of non-European origin unless transported in ships flying the English flag. This law lingered until 1849. A similar policy was followed in France.

Liberalism

A strong reaction against mercantilist attitudes began to take shape toward the middle of the 18th century. In France, the economists, known as physiocrats, demanded liberty of production and trade. In England, Economist Adam Smith demonstrated in his book *The Wealth of Nations* (1776) the advantages of removing trade restrictions. Economists and businessmen voiced their opposition to excessively high and often prohibitive customs duties and urged the negotiation of trade agreements with foreign powers. This change in attitudes led to the signing of a number of agreements embodying the new liberal ideas about trade; among them was the Anglo-French Treaty of 1786, which ended what had been an economic war between the two countries. After Adam Smith, the basic tenets of mercantilism were no longer considered defensible. This did not, however, mean that nations abandoned all mercantilist policies. Restrictive economic policies were now justified by the claim that, up to a certain point, the government should keep foreign merchandise off the domestic market in order to shelter national production from outside competition. To this end, customs levies were introduced in increasing number, replacing outright bans on imports, which became less and less frequent.

Resurgence of Protectionism

A reaction in favor of protection spread throughout the Western world in the latter part of the 19th century. Germany adopted a systematically protectionist policy and was soon followed by most other nations. Shortly after 1860, during the Civil War, the United States raised its duties sharply; the McKinley Tariff Act of 1890 was ultra-protectionist. The United Kingdom was the only country to remain faithful to the principles of free trade.

But the protectionism of the last quarter of the 19th century was mild as compared to the mercantilist policies that had been common in the 17th century and were to be revived between the two world wars. Extensive economic liberty prevailed by 1913. Quantitative restrictions were unheard of, and customs duties were low and stable. Currencies were freely convertible into gold, which in effect was a common international money. Balance-of-payments problems were few. People who wished to settle and work in a country could go where they wished with few restrictions; they could open businesses, enter trade, or export capital freely. Equal opportunity to compete was the general rule, the sole exception being the existence of limited customs preferences between certain countries, most usually between a home country and its colonies. Trade was freer throughout the Western world in 1913 than it was in Europe in 1970.

The "New" Mercantilism

World War I wrought havoc on these orderly trading conditions. By the end of the hostilities, world trade had been disrupted to a degree that made recovery very difficult. The first five years of the postwar period were marked by the dismantling of wartime controls. An economic downturn in 1920, followed by the commercial advantages that accrued to the countries whose currencies had depreciated (as had Germany's), prompted many countries to impose new trade restrictions. The resulting protectionist tide engulfed the world economy, not because policy makers consciously adhered to any specific theory but because of nationalist ideologies and the pressure of economic conditions. In an attempt to end the continual raising of customs barriers, the League of Nations organized the first World Economic Conference in May 1927. Twenty-nine countries, including the main industrial countries, subscribed to an international convention that was the most minutely detailed and balanced multilateral trade agreement approved to date. It was a precursor of the arrangements made under the General Agreement on Tariffs and Trade (GATT) of 1947.

However, the 1927 agreement remained practically without effect. During the Great Depression of the 1930s, unemployment in major countries reached unprecedented levels and engendered an epidemic of protectionist measures. Countries attempted to shore up their balance of payments by raising their customs duties and introducing a range of import quotas or even import prohibitions, accompanied by exchange controls.

From 1933 onward, the recommendations of all the postwar economic conferences based on the fundamental postulates of economic liberalism were ignored. The planning of foreign trade came to be considered a normal function of the state. Mercantilist policies dominated the world scene until after World War II, when trade agreements and supranational organizations became the chief means of managing and promoting international trade.

The Modern Theory of International Trade
Comparative-advantage Analysis

The British school of classical economics began in no small measure as a reaction against the inconsistencies of mercantilist thought. Adam Smith was the 18th-century founder of this school; as mentioned above, his famous work, *The Wealth of Nations* (1776), is in part an anti-mercantilist tract. In the book, Smith emphasized the importance of specialization as a source of increased output, and he treated international trade as a particular instance of specialization: in a world where productive resources are scarce and human wants cannot be completely satisfied, each nation should specialize in the production of goods it is particularly well-equipped to produce; it should export part of this production, taking in exchange other goods that it cannot so readily turn out.

Amplification of the Theory

The major purpose of the theory of comparative advantage is to illustrate the gains from international trade. Each country benefits by specializing in those occupations it is relatively efficient in; each should export part of that production and take, in exchange, those goods in whose production it is, for whatever reason, at a comparative disadvantage. The theory of comparative advantage thus provides a strong argument for free trade—and indeed for more of a laissez-faire attitude with respect to trade. Based on this uncomplicated example, the supporting argument is simple: specialization and free exchange among nations yield higher real income for the participants.

Sources of Comparative Advantage

During the 20th century, international economists offered a number of theories in an effort to explain why countries have differences in productivity—the factor that determines comparative advantage and the pattern of international trade.

Natural Resources

First, countries can have an advantage because they are richly endowed with a particular natural resource. For example, countries with plentiful oil resources can generally produce oil inexpensively. Because Saudi Arabia produces oil very cheaply, it holds a comparative advantage in oil, and it exports oil in order to finance imports. Similarly, countries with large areas of forests generally are the major exporters of wood, paper, and paper products. The supply available for export also depends on domestic demand. Canada has large quantities of lumber available for export to the United States, not only because of its large areas of forest but also because its small population consumes little of the supply, leaving much of the lumber available for export. Climate is another natural resource that provides an export advantage. Thus, for example, bananas are exported by Central American countries—not Iceland or Finland.

Factor Endowments: The Heckscher-Ohlin Theory

Simply put, countries with plentiful natural resources will generally have a comparative advantage in products using those resources. A related, but much more subtle, assertion was put forward by two Swedish economists, Eli Heckscher and Bertil Ohlin. Ohlin's work was built upon that of Heckscher. In recognition of his ideas as described in his path-breaking book *Interregional and International Trade* (1933), Ohlin was a recipient of the Nobel Prize for Economic Sciences in 1977.

The Heckscher-Ohlin theory focuses on the two most important factors of production, labor and capital. Some countries are relatively well-endowed with capital; the typical worker has plenty of machinery and equipment to assist with the work. In such countries, wage rates generally are high; as a result, the costs of producing labor-intensive goods—such as textiles, sporting goods, and simple consumer electronics—tend to be higher than in countries with plentiful labor and low wage rates. On the other hand, goods requiring much capital and only a little labor (automobiles and chemicals, for example) tend to be relatively inexpensive in countries with plentiful and cheap capital. Thus, countries with abundant capital should generally be able to produce capital-intensive goods relatively inexpensively, exporting them in order to pay for imports of Labor-intensive goods.

In the Heckscher-Ohlin theory, it is not the absolute amount of capital that is important; rather, it is the amount of capital per worker. A small country like Luxembourg has much less capital in total than India, but Luxembourg has more capital per worker. Accordingly, the Heckscher-Ohlin theory predicts that Luxembourg will export capital-intensive products to India and import labor-intensive products in return.

Despite its plausibility, the Heckscher-Ohlin theory is frequently at variance with the actual patterns of international trade. As an explanation of what countries actually export and import, it is much less accurate than the more obvious and straightforward natural resource theory.

One early study of the Heckscher-Ohlin theory was carried out by Wassily Leontief, a Russian-born US economist. Leontief observed that the United States was relatively well-endowed with capital. According to the theory, therefore, the United States should export capital-intensive goods and import labor-intensive ones. He found that the opposite was in fact the case: US exports are generally more labor-intensive than the type of products that the United States imports. Because his findings were the opposite of those predicted by the theory, they are known as the Leontief Paradox.

Economies of Large-scale Production

Even if countries have quite similar climates and factor endowments, they may still find it advantageous to trade. Indeed, economically similar countries often carry on a large and thriving trade. The prosperous industrialized countries have become one another's best customers. A main reason for this situation lies in what is called the economies of large-scale production (*otherwise known as* economy of scale).

For many products, there are advantages in producing on a large scale; costs become lower as more is produced. Thus, for example, automobiles can be made more cheaply in a factory producing 100,000 units than in a small factory producing only 1,000 units. This means that countries have an incentive to specialize in the manufacture of specific products in order to reduce costs. To sell a large volume of output, they may have to look to export markets.

The smaller the country, and the more limited its domestic market, the more incentive it has to look to international trade as a way of gaining the advantages of large-scale production. Thus, Luxembourg or Belgium has much more to gain, relatively, than the United States. Indeed, the advantages of large-scale production were one of the major sources of gain from the establishment of the European Economic Community (EEC, ultimately replaced by the European Union), which was formed for the purpose of providing free trade between most western European countries.

Even a large country such as the United States, however, can gain in some cases by exporting in order to exploit the economies of production lines. For example, the Boeing Company has been able to produce airplanes more efficiently and cheaply because it is able to sell large numbers of aircraft to other countries. The importing countries also gain because they can buy aircraft abroad at prices far lower than they would pay for domestically produced equivalents.

Technology

Technological development can also provide a distinctive trade advantage. The relatively advanced countries—particularly the United States, Japan, and those of western Europe—have been the principal exporters of high-technology products, such as computers and precision machinery.

One important aspect of technology is that it can change rapidly. This is perhaps most obvious in the computer field, where productivity has increased and costs have fallen sharply since the early 1960s (*see* Moore's law). Such rapid changes present several challenges. For countries that are not in the front rank, it raises the question of whether they should import high-technology products or attempt to enter the circle of the most advanced nations. For the countries that have held the technological lead in the past, there is always the possibility that they will be overtaken by newcomers. This occurred in the second half of the 20th century, when Japan advanced technologically in its automobile production to the point where it could challenge the automobile leadership of North America and Europe. Japan quickly became the world's foremost producer of automobiles, and, by the early 21st century, Korean automakers were following the Japanese example with the aggressive export of automobiles.

Technological advances also strengthen global trade in a general sense: e-commerce, for example, reduced the impact of geographic distance by facilitating fast, efficient, real-time ties between businesses and individuals around the world. Indeed, at the end of the 20th century, information technology, an industry that scarcely existed 20 years earlier, exceeded the combined world trade in agriculture, automobiles, and textiles.

The Product Cycle

The spread of technology across national boundaries means that comparative advantage can change. The most technologically advanced countries generally have the advantage in making new products, but as time passes, other countries may gain the advantage. For example, many television sets were produced in the United States during the 1950s. As time passed, however, and technological change in the television industry became less rapid, there was less advantage in producing sets in the United States. Producers of television sets had an incentive to look to other locations with lower wage rates. In time, the manufacturers established overseas operations in Taiwan, Hong Kong, Korea, and elsewhere. Concurrently, the United States turned to new activities, such as the manufacture of supercomputers, the development of computer software, and new applications of satellite technology.

Benefits of Trade

The benefits of trade are unquestionable. For consumers, global trade lowers prices. In addition, it introduces far greater product variety, allowing consumers to choose a broader range of goods and services.

Global trade also offers benefits to businesses and their workers. Firms exposed to global trade competition are also exposed to the world's best practices in areas such as supply chain management, production processes, technology, and finance. Studies show that firms exposed to the world's best practices demonstrate higher productivity. Likewise, trade promotes greater worker productivity, which in turn drives workers' standard of living. Productivity growth of just 1.4% per year means average living standards take 50 years to double. If a faster rate of 2.9% per year is attained, living standards take just 24 years to double.

Studies have estimated that the annual payoff from US trade liberalization following World War II created a benefit of five thousand dollars per capita or three thousand dollars for an average American family of four. Another study reports that a reduction of remaining barriers on trade and services could generate over $1.5 trillion in income for the world. Likewise, reducing trade barriers on agriculture and manufactured goods could generate $250 billion of additional income to the world economy each year. While debt relief and foreign aid can help to reduce poverty, trade is a more powerful tool. For instance, in 2004, industrialized countries spent over $78 billion in development assistance to poor countries and industrialized countries provided debt relief of $56 billion. Even a modest level of trade liberalization to developing countries would have generated over $140 billion in benefits during that time. Studies show that reducing barriers to global trade has the potential to lift hundreds of millions out of poverty.

Headwinds

Despite the economic benefits of enhanced global trade, it faces many political challenges. In the West, particularly, many middle-class workers are fed up with a political and economic system. This can result in economic inequality, social instability, and, in some countries, mass immigration, even if it also led to economic growth and cheaper product.

At the same time, growing trade can exacerbate the global effect of climate change. Pollution in one part of the world leads to extreme weather events in another and the cutting of forests in the few "green lungs" left, like the Amazon rainforest, has a further devastated effect on not just the world's biodiversity, but its capacity to cope with hazardous greenhouse gases' emissions.

The Future of Global Trade

History and economic theory would suggest that trade will continue to grow. The economic benefits it offers are simply too great to turn backward. On the other hand, the growth of global trade, while likely, is not guaranteed. As we've seen in this chapter, wars, and the economic uncertainty they cause, are devastating to business in general, but particularly to global trade. Likewise, the benefits of global trade are not uniform. For trade to continue to grow, policy makers must address the economic dislocation that can affect workers who lose their jobs to more efficient factory sources. And care must be taken to ensure a level playing field with regards to our environmental standards and working conditions.

| 2 |

THE FUNDAMENTALS

"The minute you get away from fundamentals--whether its proper technique, work ethic, or mental preparation--the bottom can fall out of your game, your schoolwork, your job, whatever you're doing." - Michael Jordan

Over the years, I've had the privilege of working with a diverse range of companies to navigate through the complexities of our ever-changing global economy. Those companies that have been successful in developing a world-class supply chain and have, *without exception,* focused on four fundamentals.

Price

The desire to reduce product cost, increase profits, or maintain competitiveness generally drives interest in products sourcing or off-shore manufacturing. In other words, in a global economy, your product must be price competitive or your business is likely to perish. While lower prices alone do not make a quality supply chain, they are unquestionably a major driver.

Over the years, we have worked with our clients to obtain a low "first cost" from the factory source, as part of a transparent and highly efficient supply chain. However, we understand that what really matters is not just the first cost but also the delivered or "landed" cost of goods. This landed cost includes the first cost of the product, plus costs for shipping, insurance, and applicable customs duties. As you develop a cost-efficient supply chain, it is critical to carefully manage each of these components of your product's landed cost.

In negotiating the first cost of a product with the factory, it is important to view the world through the factory's eyes, as well as your own. Like your own business, your factory source faces its own set of challenges. This includes materials procurement, labor-cost management, production scheduling, the needs of its other customers, and the like. Therefore, it is important to approach price negotiations with the goal of establishing a "win-win" relationship that will endure. Showing concern for your factory's needs, as well as your own, will help you establish trust with your supplier. This, in turn, will help you navigate the inevitable challenges that surface in the course of a successful outsourcing relationship.

Over the years, a consistent challenge we face involves clients who purposely inflate purchase volume estimates in hope of obtaining a lower price. Such misrepresentation is seldom successful and leads to diminished trust between purchaser and seller. On the other hand, factories understand that it often takes time for a company to introduce a new product to the market and that a detailed purchasing forecast may not be possible. In our experience, it is better to communicate honest volume estimates to the factory, even if they turn out to be less than the volumes actually purchased.

Another factor that affects price is the manufacturing efficiency. Factories typically do not like to produce small volume orders, as this requires them to set up and take down production lines on a frequent basis. This, of course, is inefficient. Therefore, in order to achieve better pricing, a buyer might negotiate with a factory to make its entire annual production in one run. In exchange for this increased production efficiency, the factory might agree to store the excess production, and release it to the buyer at predetermined times throughout the year. Stated differently, the desire for greater manufacturing efficiency may prompt your factory to become an inventory partner. This strategy may be quite attractive, especially for a well-capitalized factory source.

As with your own business, payment terms and payment certainty affect price. If you can make a manufacturer feel secure that it will be paid, you are more likely to get a better price. For example, you might consider posting a bank letter of credit in favor of the factory to ensure payment of your orders. Likewise, placing a deposit while you place your order helps the factory pay its material purchasing cost. This makes the factory feel less at risk, and therefore, may result in lower pricing. On the other hand, refusing to provide a payment guarantee, or a deposit, and demanding lengthy payment terms creates uncertainty because it requires the factory to use its own capital to support your business. If the factory feels less secure and must use its capital to fund the requested payment terms, the price it quotes you could be higher.

There are multiple factors that affect product pricing. For instance, if a factory is highly experienced in making your type of product, it is more likely to offer a good price.

This experience gives the factory confidence that it can successfully manufacture the product in an efficient and predictable manner. With experience comes confidence and if the factory is confident that it can successfully manufacture a product in an efficient and predictable manner then it is willing to be more aggressive in its price quotation.

Unique product requirements such as product certification that are specific or exclusive to your market can also affect price. For example, most electrical products sold in the United States require Underwriters Laboratories listing. Obtaining UL Certification for electrical products can be both time consuming and expensive for the factory, requiring detailed product reviews, site visits and, and typically, adjustments to its manufacturing processes and record keeping. Since the certification attaches only to a specific product, the factory will understandably want to pass costs through to you, as the buyer. This inevitably affects pricing.

Another factor that can affect pricing is whether your product has unique tooling requirements. Many factories are willing to front or share in the cost of tooling (for example, injection molds) and amortize the cost of such tooling over a certain volume of production. This, naturally, affects the price quoted.

As you can see, there are multiple factors that affect negotiating the best first cost with a factory. Careful understanding of your own product specification, manufacturing processes, and the unique capabilities and capitalization of your factory are all critical factors in product price negotiations.

Product design is an often overlooked factor affecting the landed cost of your product. The amount of space taken by your product in a shipping container can dramatically affect shipping efficiency and cost. A modest tweak in design often yields dramatic cost savings. Therefore, consideration of the shipping efficiency of your product should be a key element of the product design process.

Another common mistake of importers is the inefficient use of container space. For example, it's always more efficient to "floor load" a container that can ship products on pallets. On the other hand, less labor is required to unload a container if your products are shipped on pallets. Apart from the matter of floor loading versus palletized product for shipment, many businesses fail to pack a container to its capacity. When a container is not fully packed, products in the shipping container are only stacked five or six feet high and this doesn't utilize the entire height of the container. Even though shipping efficiency does not affect your first cost from the factory, it is definitely a significant contributing factor in terms of your ability to realize the lowest possible landed cost for your product.

As noted above, price is also affected by other components of the "landed" cost for your product. Shipping is a major cost for most importers. Sophisticated buyers carefully evaluate freight forwarders based on their unique cost and service levels. They also might schedule production during seasons when shipping costs tend to be lower. Over the years, we've had success aggregating the combined shipping needs of our clients and then soliciting rate proposals from forwarders based on higher aggregated shipping volume and attention to servicing our client's unique transit routes. Negotiating shipping rates in this manner can lead to substantial savings.

Skyrocketing shipping costs during a COVID-19 pandemic highlights the importance of shipping efficiency. Prior to the pandemic, the cost of shipping a 40-foot container from Shanghai to Los Angeles averaged about $3,000. During the pandemic, it was not uncommon to see container prices for the same route exceed $15,000. These higher shipping rates dramatically raised the "landed" cost for many products. Also, it forced businesses to revisit whether they were using their shipping container space efficiently. Some businesses ceased to import products that were inefficient to ship, as they could secure the same product at a lower, landed cost from factory sources closer to home.

Transit insurance is another cost factor affecting a well-managed supply chain. I recommend against purchasing insurance by the shipment. Instead, it should be purchased on an annual basis. Purchasing insurance by the shipment is not cost effective, similar to purchasing pizza by the slice rather than by the whole pizza. Shipping rates are affected by factors other than shipping volume routes. For example, a sophisticated insurer will want to evaluate your factory relationship, a payment term, and the contractual provisions that adhere to your factory relationships. As explained in Chapter 5, having in place good contracts with your supplier allows your insurance underwriter to assess which party is responsible for product quality, shipping delays, and it also should specify when title transfers. These factors, in turn, empower your insurer to maintain a lower insurance premium for your products in transit.

Quality

Achieving and maintaining product quality lies at the core of sophisticated manufacturing. And consistent product quality is fundamental to your having a successful supply chain. While price and quality tend to be inversely related, careful quality control standards and procedures can ensure quality product at competitive prices.

Maintaining product quality involves multiple factors:

Factory Selection

The first step to making a quality product is to find a quality factory. Factory capabilities and qualifications must be carefully evaluated. Depending on the type of product being made, the factory may need to satisfy certain certification requirements (for example, FDA certifications). Also, manufacturing process certifications (e.g. ISO) are an indicator of factory expertise and manufacturing consistency. In every case, the factory needs to have the capacity to operate efficiently to meet and exceed your expectations. Sophisticated businesses do not purchase products from a factory that they have not personally visited. By visiting your factory, you can assess its capabilities firsthand, using a detailed factory audit checklist.

Factories should be carefully evaluated for manufacturing competency and ability to deliver product at a price, quality, and on a delivery schedule that meets your needs. In addition, the factory should be the "right" size. In other words, your orders must be meaningful to the factory in order for you to retain its focus and support.

In addition, the in-person visit allows you to assess the factory's owner and key staff and begin the important process of establishing personal relationships. Over the years, I've developed a mental checklist that has served me well in factory selection. First, I look for a factory that manufactures products for brands that are known to be high quality. For example, an electronics factory that manufactures for Japanese brands is likely to be high quality, as Japanese buyers are notoriously picky and quality conscious. Second, I look for a factory whose owner is actively involved in the business. This ensures, when an issue arrives, you will have the opportunity to address your concerns with someone empowered to make a prompt decision. Third, I always look for a "watchmaker" personality—a key employee or owner who is passionately dedicated to making outstanding products. A few years ago, I visited a factory we were teaching to make a medical device, that included a latex bladder. It was important that the bladder released air at a specified rate through holes the size of a small pin prick. Some initial samples received from the factory had not met this standard and during the morning of our factory visit, we had shared with factory representatives our disappointment. As is often the case, the morning meeting was followed by lunch nearby the factory. During lunch, I noticed that one of the key employees had not joined the larger group. When we returned to the factory after lunch, I spotted the employee outside the factory near a large washbasin, where he was testing the bladders by dunking them into the water and watching for air bubbles. Later in the afternoon, he rejoined the meeting, very pleased to have developed a solution to the problem we discussed that morning. He also shared several other ideas for improving the product, which were spot on. Based on that interaction, I knew that the factory was committed to the project and determined to make a superior product. The fact is, they could have conducted leak testing during the week after the factory visit and reported an issue later on. However, the fact that they were bothered by their failure to make the product as specified proved to me that they would become a trustworthy partner.

In addition, an increasingly important aspect of factory selection involves establishing redundancy. As we discuss below in the section on risk management, factory selection also ideally involves the allocation of your production to more than one factory. This, of course, can involve more management of the manufacturing process on your part. On the other hand, in an ever-changing international trade environment, diversifying your factory risk can be as important as your decision of whether a factory can a deliver a product to you at the desired price and quality and on the required delivery timeline.

Product Specifications and Inspections

Once a qualified and reliable factory is identified, it is important that detailed product, packaging, and quality control specifications are clearly communicated to the factory. In addition to these three areas, it is equally important to provide specification tolerance information to the factory with classifications noting the acceptable quality levels (generally classified as major, minor, or critical). These will be critical to the success of a quality control inspection.

Every quality control inspection requires a checklist, which provides a guidance to the inspector on how each component is checked and tested. An inspection usually includes the following:

- Appearance and workmanship
- Testing for function and performance
- Labeling quantity verification

Inspections can be conducted at various times throughout the production process and also should be conducted prior to shipment, depending on your requirements. There are three main types of product quality inspections:

Pre-Production Inspections. These are conducted before production starts. These inspections can help ensure the quality of raw materials and efficient factory setup.

During-Production Inspections. These are conducted while production is in process. These inspections can help in catching raw material substitutions and defects early on in the manufacturing process. This, in turn, can help avoid delays to remake nonconforming goods. During-productions inspections are important to address a common source of quality problems. A tried-and-true way for a factory to increase its profits once the price of a product is set is to cheapen the materials used to make the product. Sadly, this practice is all too common and requires constant vigilance. When negotiating your factory relationship, you should ensure that you have the right for your quality inspection team be present during production in order to identify substituted raw materials early on, before they can be incorporated into your products.

Pre-Shipment Inspections. These are the most common type of inspections. These inspections are conducted when the goods are 100% produced and at least 80% packaged. Once the inspection is completed, an inspection report is prepared and sent to the customer for review. For purposes of accountability, the report should be certified by the inspector. Also, it should include detailed findings on each of the QC checklist criteria.

Packaging. Packaging is essential to product quality. If a product is damaged in transit due to poor packaging, all the quality inspections performed prior to or during production or prior to shipment become largely irrelevant.

There are three main checkpoints for packaging quality control. As with product components, factories can save money relative to the price quoted by utilizing inferior quality packaging materials. A common example of this is the use of flimsy cartons, which break down in humid environments or lose their structural integrity during shipment. This can make products difficult to manage in your distribution facility or the distribution facility of your customer. Recognizing this problem, many large retailers either reject shipments containing damaged cartons or charge back the cost of the product or the extra handling costs to repackage it. Like quality issues relating to your product itself, quality issues relating to packaging typically reflect the failure of a business to properly specify their packaging from the outset and then carefully monitor products that are actually shipped.

Shipping Carton Standard. The standard for a shipping carton should be based on the weight and size of the products it contains. Carton strength should be specified, typically using the Box Maker's Certificate (BMC), a round stamp on the bottom of the box with detailed information regarding the box's strength. Although the BMC is not legally required, it is proof that the box has been properly tested and rated.

In specifying your shipping carton standard, you need to consider the stacked weight of your products in a container. Obviously, it takes a strong box to hold the weight of multiple layers of stacked boxes. In addition, keep in mind that most cartons are loaded and unloaded from a container or a truck multiple times before being sold to the ultimate consumer. The number of times you expect your product to be handled prior to a container being open is another critical factor affecting your box specifications.

Another obvious factor affecting container specifications is how full you anticipate filling each container. For example, if you leave space at the top of each carton rather than filling it to the brim, it is more likely the carton will collapse under the weight of multiple cartons stacked on top of it.

Sealing Method and Packaging Materials. Depending on the type of product, it may need to be packaged securely and safely to maintain its structural integrity against external elements (temperature, humidity, shipping, and handling) during transit. The quality control checklist should confirm that all packaging requirements (e.g., bulk or individually packaged with the use of poly bags as a liner or sealed for retail-ready) are followed.

A few years ago, I witnessed the effect that humidity has on the cartons stored in tropical conditions. On behalf of one of our clients, we had successfully negotiated its factory becoming an inventory partner (i.e., large quantities of product were made in advance and stored at the factory, allowing our client to pull from the inventory in order to achieve shorter delivery times). During one of my visits to the factory, I asked to see our client's stored inventory. I remember it was a sweltering August day and the near daily thunderstorms ensured high levels of humidity. When we looked at the products at the warehouse, we noticed that almost every stack of boxes on a pallet tilted one way or another. Upon further inspection, it became evident that the factory had utilized cartons that were not structurally sound and lost strength in a humid environment. As a result, it was necessary to repackage all of the products prior to shipment. As a corrective action plan, the factory agreed to delay boxing of future inventory until closer to the date at which it would be shipped.

This is obviously a mistake that was easy to correct. However, correction would have been much more challenging and expensive if our client had allowed the shipment of products packed in mushy boxes that fell of their pallets when unloaded by its customer. At best, this would have resulted in an unhappy customer, but more likely it would have resulted in a serious charge-back to compensate the customer for extra cost associated with managing poorly packaged goods.

The quality control checklist for packaging should also include a section detailing the types of packaging materials used for inner cartons, internal packaging, and shipping cartons. The types of packing materials can vary from Styrofoam peanuts, bubble wraps, foam, air pillows, or just large sheets of paper.

It is worth noting at this point that minimizing packaging materials is both good business and good for customer relations. By definition, if you design your products so that they require less packaging, you obviously can ship more of them in a container. As discussed in the previous section, shipping efficiency can have a major impact on the landed cost of your products. So, less tends to be better. On the other hand, less is also better with many of today's consumers who are motivated to purchase products that use less packaging and, therefore, generate less waste. Reduced use of packaging material is one way to "Go Green."

When the shipping cartons are stacked on a pallet, it is important that the proper strapping and shrink-wrapping be applied to ensure the cartons do not slip off the pallets during transit.

As noted above, the decision whether to ship your products "floor loaded" or on pallets affects both shipping efficiency and the cost of managing your products at a distribution center upon receipt. Most factories are motivated to floor load your product because this obviously results in more units per container (and possibly a larger order for them). On the other hand, depending on your product, the time and labor required to unload a full loaded container of products can be either impractical or unnecessarily expensive. Therefore, the decision on how to load your container is one that affects the overall cost of your business as well as those of your customer. As such, it deserves careful attention.

If you elect to ship your products on pallets, how cartons are organized and affixed to the pallet will have a major impact on the condition of your products upon arrival. Because of that, most businesses either shrink-wrap the cartons on their container and/or strap them to the pallet to avoid shifting in transit.

Shipping Markings and Barcodes

An importer will encounter shipping delays if carton markings or barcodes are incorrect, missing, or illegible. Omitting or incorrectly labeling packaging can lead to major problems at US or foreign customs.

All goods imported into the United States must be marked with their country of origin. In addition, there are several other important markings that are commonly included on shipping cartons, they are:

- Purchaser's name/brand
- Purchaser's order number (PO#)
- Item number and product description
- Carton dimensions
- Weight (Net weight and gross weight if required)
- Number of cartons within one shipment ("1 of 20," "2 of 20," etc.)
- Country of origin
- Any warning labels and icons (e.g., "fragile," "hazardous materials," "this side up," etc.)

If used on shipping cartons, barcodes need to be printed clearly using the correct size and orientation for easy scanning and timely processing when goods are delivered. Here are a few issues that can impair barcode function:

- Poor printing of barcode
- Locating the barcode too close to the edge of the label or too close to other text or symbols
- Damage or distortion of barcode
- Oversized or undersized printing of barcode
- Wrong orientation code

Ensuring quality products is multi-faceted. It involves selection of a quality factory, clear communication of product and packaging specifications, and careful development and implementation of quality control procedures.

In my experience, quality problems typically trace back to poor factory selection, failure to communicate clear specifications and tolerances, and lack of attention to production management.

As noted above, it is imperative that for each product, you develop concrete specifications, acceptable tolerances, and detailed quality control inspection checklists. In addition, quality should be confirmed at various points: prior to production, delivery, and prior to shipment either by you or an independent third party with expertise in your type of product. Finally, part of onboarding a factory source should include execution of a manufacturing agreement that places clear responsibility for product quality on the factory and provides meaningful redress if quality expectations are not satisfied.

Delivery

Low-priced, quality products are of little value if they are not delivered on time. The COVID-19 pandemic has highlighted the consequences for a business when delivery of its products—or components used to make its products—are delayed. Experience suggests that the best way to ensure timely delivery involves careful selection of factory sources, paying close attention to management of the factory production process, and careful planning of shipments.

Over the years, we have developed strategies to ensure timely deliveries of products. These strategies focus on the main causes of delayed delivery. Delays on the part of the factory and sourcing materials, delays in production, and delays in shipping your products once production is complete. In your initial factory selection process, it is important to understand whether your factory is reliant upon others to supply key components and, if it is, the strength of its relationship with those suppliers. An example of a challenge faced by businesses currently involves the desire to relocate manufacturing from China to other locations. It is often possible to find a factory at an alternative country (such as Vietnam) capable of making your product, but that factory may be reliant upon China to supply key raw materials. This should in turn trigger an inquiry on your part as to the reliability of the alternative factory's supply chain.

A second cause of delivery delay involves inefficiency of production by your selected factory. At the time you review the factory's quotations for product, your full attention should be paid to its projected production lead times. As you consider the implications of those lead times for your own supply chain, it is prudent to know the factory's lead time to avoid disruptions if production is delayed. In addition, it is important your manufacturing agreement includes penalties for late delivery, as this will motivate the factory prioritize the on-time production of your products.

The third major cause of delayed delivery involves shipping delays. Moreover, the delay in materials' procurement or production is often compounded by the need to reschedule shipping, as it's uncommon for shipping lines to have a vessel between your ports of departure and arrival more than one time of the week. Therefore, missing that delivery by a single day may result in a four- or five-day delay until your cargo can catch the next vessel.

To address these common causes of delivery delay, you should consider providing the factory with an advance forecast, which allows the factory to preorder materials from its own suppliers, timing their arrival to coincide with your production timeline. In addition, in many cases, we have been able to arrange for a factory to premake product and become an inventory partner, thereby dramatically reducing overall delivery times, since ordering and production by the factory has already been completed.

An obvious factor affecting delivery times is the means of transportation chosen. This is affected by a couple factors including whether to ship by ocean or by air, whether (if they are shipped by ocean) they are shipped directly or through an intermediary port, whether the vessel on which they are shipped is a "fast" or "slow" boat, whether there are backlogs at the port of export or arrival, and whether there is an efficient transfer from the port of entry to the ultimate destination. Management of an efficient supply chain requires developing a strong relationship with your freight forwarder and maintaining regular communication to ensure timely deliveries in the face of ever-changing circumstances.

The importance of maintaining relationships with multiple freight forwarders and port authorities was highlighted in a project we managed several years ago, with the shipment of seasonally harvested, perishable trees from the United States to China. Due to the unique biology of the tree varieties we were involved in shipping, we knew that we had approximately 38 days from the date a tree was dug from the ground and soil washed from its roots, shipped in a refrigerated container to its destination and replanted. Obviously, there was little room for error in this process, and shipments were further complicated by the need to comply with government regulations and permits applicable to the shipment of trees. Moreover, the exact shipping date for the products was affected by springtime weather, since the trees could not be harvested under certain weather conditions but needed to be replanted before the weather grew warm in spring. As if this project were not challenging enough, two weeks before we were scheduled to begin shipping trees, the West Coast dockworkers went on strike, which slowed container movement to a crawl. To manage this crisis, our team reached out to multiple shipping lines and port authorities by ports with the least congestion. In addition, we developed alternative routing through Vancouver, Canada, which allowed us to avoid the worst consequences of the US strike. On the strength of being nimble and having in place long term relationships, we were able to deliver the trees on a timely basis, and they were successfully planted within the 38-day window.

Risk Management

While most experts agree that a supply chain should focus on price, quality, and delivery, many overlook how critical it is to manage risk, both from outset of establishing your supply chain and on ongoing basis.

Because global trade is by its very nature "international" business, outcomes are affected by factors not necessarily present in your local market. For example, when establishing your supply chain, it is important to evaluate political or country risk. For example, most businesses are disinclined to purchase products from Afghanistan or Libya, as those countries' governments are known to be unstable. Likewise, many developing countries are subject to political changes that make business operations challenging. Therefore, where you manufacture your product is a critical element of risk management.

In addition to managing risk from the outset, sophisticated businesses also work to diversify risk. For example, companies that make their products at factory sources in more than one country are better positioned to manage country risk.

In recent years, imposition of tariffs has dramatically affected the efficiency of many supply chains. Tariffs, of course, directly affect the "landed" cost of your product. In addition, whether, when, and the amount of a tariff injects uncertainty into your supply chain. Therefore, as with country or political risk, businesses that can diversify factory sources across the multiple countries or regions are better positioned to manage tariff risk.

One of the more significant disruptions to international trade and recent years involved tariffs imposed by the Trump Administration on many products from China. Overnight, many businesses experienced a dramatic increase in the price of their products or the components used in the manufacture of their products. This either forced businesses to raise prices, absorb the tariffs in the form of lower profits, or force their manufacturers to share in the cost of the tariffs. Part of what made the "Trump Tariffs" so disruptive was that they ran counter to the past 70 years of global trade policy, which was characterized by the ongoing *reduction* of trade barriers. Since the tariffs were focused on China only, companies were incentivized to identify alternative suppliers outside of China. While that is certainly possible, the time and expense required was a major disruption for many companies.

Apart from one's view of the efficacy of the Trump Tariffs, they certainly highlighted the value to your business of having a diversified supplier base capable of helping you manage "country political risk." Businesses that successfully relocated supply chains outside of China prospered relative to those who had not considered country and political risk.

Pandemics and climate change are another obvious part of supply chain risk. An unpredictable weather event can affect the reliability of your supply chain, as do outbreaks of disease, which can slow production and transportation of goods.

Shipping prices and timelines are also another major risk factor. In response to the COVID-19 pandemic, there is growing interest in "nearshoring" as a means of mitigating shipping cost increases and delays.

Diversification is the key to managing the inherent risks of any supply chain. Just like managing an investment portfolio, it is prudent to spread production across multiple factories and countries and bring it closer to home if possible.

Even businesses who carefully manage risk throughout their supply chain cannot afford all risks. Murphy's Law is one of the truest laws of nature: "Anything that can go wrong will go wrong." Who, for example, would have predicted the massive Evergreen container ship would get stuck in the Suez Canal? Likewise, in 2019, virtually no one saw the COVID-19 pandemic coming.

Nonetheless, the fact that risk exists in the world does not mean that risks should not be taken. For example, most of us drive or walk to work each day, which involves an undisputable risk of death! While international trade involves inherent risks, the benefits are simply too attractive to avoid taking such risks. The key, however, is to carefully plan your supply chain and pay close attention to changing circumstances.

As discussed in this chapter, sourcing a product involves, like any business, certain fundamentals. Businesses that successfully establish efficient and resilient supply chains focus relentlessly on price, quality, delivery, and risk management. While no businessperson control factors like wars, tariffs, pandemics, and weather, careful focus on these fundamentals will help you succeed where others fail.

Case Study: Medical Device Manufacturer

In 2009 a private equity firm ("PE Firm") purchased a manufacturer of a premium quality medical device. While the manufacturer's product was of the highest quality, its manufacturing cost was too high, making it difficult for the manufacturer to grow sales and market share. As part of its post-acquisition business strategy, the PE firm desired to do offshore production of the medical device to reduce its cost. But it needed to do so in a manner that didn't sacrifice product quality and also complied with strict FDA regulations applicable to the device.

Prior to the PE firm contacting us, it had a bad experience with an agent it had hired to assist it with manufacturing the medical device in China. That agent had found a factory source for the PE firm but refused to reveal the factory source and had been taking money under the table from the factory. This made the PE firm feel that its supply chain was at risk, and it also assumed that it was not receiving the best possible, first cost from the factory.

As a result, when we entered into the relationship, our client's trust with manufacturing in China was at a low point. From the outset, we worked closely with the client to make sure that the supply chain we created would be fully transparent and offer the first-cost price from the factory.

Fortunately, because the company acquired by the PE firm had manufactured the medical device for several years, it could provide us with samples and detailed drawings of the device. In addition, employees who stayed on following the acquisition had extensive experience manufacturing the device prior to the acquisition. Supported by this product knowledge and technical expertise, our team identified multiple factory sources within about three weeks. Based on samples and drawings provided by our client, we were able to get preliminary quotations from both factories that promised dramatic cost savings for our client.

One source had expertise factoring the inner workings of the device. The other had expertise in manufacturing textile used on the exterior of the device that had contact with the patient's skin. Neither, however, had expertise in making a complete product similar to the one our client desired to manufacture. In short, we knew that successfully sourcing the device would require us to commit to considerable training of both factories.

With that in mind, we arranged for one of our client's experts to travel with me and our in-country team to visit both factories. During each visit, we shared details of the device, assessed the factory's capabilities, and coached their management on new manufacturing techniques that would shore up their respective deficiencies. Our team also worked closely with each factory to help it make appropriate registrations with the FDA and to understand the specific manufacturing and record-keeping requirement for FDA products.

The sampling phase with each factory was extensive. Adjustments were made in both the manufacturing process used in making the medical device and to its materials. Nonetheless, each round of samples was better than the one before, until after approximately three rounds of samples, the client was sufficiently satisfied to place an initial order.

Before placing the initial order, however, we worked with the factory to ensure the packaging of the medical device had an attractive appearance consistent with the premium quality of the product itself. This required detailed specification of packaging for each medical device, detailed specification of cardboard boxes, the provision of direction on how boxes should be how they were stacked for transport, and other various instructions. In addition, we worked with the factories to carefully track manufacturing lot numbers as required by the FDA. (The use of manufacturing lot numbers allows defective production to be quickly identified and isolated.)

Based on our client's extensive knowledge of its medical device, the knowledge we gave by sampling and commercialization of the process, we were able to work with the client and the factory to develop a detailed QC checklist. This checklist was utilized in conducting quality control inspections on all medical devices prior to shipment by the factory.

Now that the product samples and packaging had been approved, we began production of the first orders. Initial orders from each factory were small—only a single 20 ft. container. This allowed the client to validate that production be consistent with the sample quality and transportation logistics before placing larger orders. Within a couple months of the initial production, our client was purchasing over four containers of the product a month between the two factories.

As a result of our work for the client, its landed cost of product was reduced by over 35%. This allowed it to rationalize the pricing of its product in the market, resulting in dramatic growth of its business and its success in gaining market share for its products. Over time, it developed a collaborative relationship with its factories, leading to incremental quality improvements in the medical device over time. As trust developed between our client and its factory, the factory began to be an inventory partner, holding two to three containers of extra stock at the factories to essentially reduce production lead times to zero once an order was placed.

As you can see, throughout the process, we focused relentlessly on lower cost, premium quality, on-time delivery, and management of risk.

| 3 |

THE PRODUCT SOURCING PROCESS

"To begin with the end in mind means to start with a clear understanding of your destination. It means to know where you're going so that you better understand where you are now and so that the steps you take are always in the right direction." –Stephen R. Covey

Across products and industries, the product sourcing process is remarkably similar. In other words, the key steps to sourcing or manufacturing a medical device, a motor, or a lampshade are more or less the same.

Product Design

As an initial step to establishing your offshore manufacturing supply chain, you will need to have a product design. Ideally, this would include a bill of materials, design drawings, and even a proto-type or sample of the product you desire to make. Or maybe you're seeking to outsource an existing product, in which case you likely also have samples of current production.

Information regarding your product design should be carefully reviewed to evaluate where the best sourcing options are (e.g., which country, what type of factory), what regulatory compliance may be required, what customs duties are applicable, and the like. For example, most countries have types of products for which they are well known—products for which they have appropriate natural resources, manufacturing experience and efficiencies, and expertise. Examples would include wood products from Vietnam or cotton goods from Egypt. Likewise, depending on the type of product, selecting a factory having specific certifications (such as a factory certified to make FDA products or UL certified products) can be essential.

Also, as part of a product's design review, it's often possible to substitute materials in a manner that can result in significant customs duty savings. Or to adjust the amount of assembly (think importing components vs. a completely assembled product) to minimize customs duty.

During the product design review, careful attention should be given to shipping efficiencies for the product. Often minor tweaks to a product can help it to better "nest" for shipping purposes. Such design adjustments can dramatically reduce shipping costs.

A few years ago a business had designed a pot to grow plants. For shipping, the pots were placed one inside the other in long stacks, which in turn were placed on pallets loaded into a container. The shape of the pot, however, did allow another pot to nest inside it with the bottom of one pot touching another. As a result, shipping efficiency of the pots was approximately 25% below the optimum level. By redesigning the pot to allow it to nest more efficiently, the customer reduced its freight cost by approximately 20% more than paying for the cost of modifying the product to make it ship more efficiently, and materially lowering its landed cost for the product.

Factory Selection

Factory selection is key to manufacturing a product that meets price, quality, and delivery expectations while simultaneously managing risk. Selecting the right factory is akin to building your entire supply chain on a solid foundation. Choosing the right factory is like choosing a good business partner: it should be done carefully and with a long-term time horizon in mind.

To successfully identify a good factory source, you should first source and evaluate several options, ideally in more than one country. To do this, you should conduct a comprehensive audit of each factory's capabilities. As part of the audit, you should seek to understand what other customers the factory manufactures for, as this is typically an indicator of factory quality.

As noted above, a shorthand approach to evaluating factory quality is to inquire about the factory's other customers. If, for example, factory manufacturers for leading Japanese brands, the factory likely has well developed internal procedures and pays close attention to detail. Japanese businesses are notorious for being sticklers for product quality. As a result, if your factory makes products for such companies, you may be able to "freeride" on the work done by others.

Primarily due to advances in technology, product sampling and developed timelines have been dramatically reduced. Years ago, a business often had never seen its product until arrival of the sample. On the sample arrival date, much like Christmas, all of those involved in the development of a product crowded around the conference room table to analyze each sample. Today, with enhanced communication technology, samples are often initially made using 3D CAD software within an initial review occurring by video conference. 3D printing has also made it possible for a client to view a sample long before committing to a mold for the products, which can often be a large expense. This is described in more detail in the section below.

Once the preliminary audit is complete, you should personally visit the factory, review the product with the factory's management, and obtain a preliminary price quotation. During this process, we are especially focused on evaluating the factory's owners and key managers. For example, do they seem dedicated to building quality products and meeting customer expectations? Do they have a passion for what they do? Do their employees seem to enjoy working? Will your production be meaningful for the factory, or are your orders at risk of being lost amongst orders placed by other customers?

As part of the factory selection process, we also require the factory to enter into a manufacturing agreement that clearly defines the parties' responsibilities and creates accountability for the factory for defective products and late deliveries. Setting clear expectations of the factory early on avoids countless challenges later on.

Product Development

Once you've settled on the design of a product, attention must be given to converting that design into a commercially viable product. This requires an understanding of manufacturing techniques and processes. The product development process is also driven by price considerations and often leads to compromises that allow the manufacturer to adjust product prices that meet consumer expectations.

The tradeoffs involved in commercialization of a product often involve a creative tension in between product designers and product developers, the latter being the team responsible for converting the design into a product that can be manufactured efficiently and to a high-quality standard while meeting designated consumer price points. This process typically involves the substitution of lower cost materials, materials that are easier to manage consistency of in production, and manufacturing processes that better control quality. A recent example that comes to mind involves the production of glass shades. As designed, the product made was "opal" glass, which involves the manufacturing process where the glass is blown individually and is therefore inherently inconsistent. Because this involves wasting of materials in the manufacturing process (to reject glass shades that don't meet specifications), it is relatively inefficient and therefore more expensive. By contrast, case glass looks virtually identical to opal glass, but it is manufactured using a more organized process. As a result, the product is more consistent, there is less waste, and, therefore, cost is lower. Over time, the company's product developers won out over its designers because using case glass allowed them to achieve a lower cost and a more consistent product that had virtually the same appearance of opal glass.

Product Sampling

Once one or more factories are selected, a business will order samples of the product for review. Typically, a factory will make a sample at no charge, viewing this as a cost of doing business. On the other hand, factories typically expect the customer to pay for shipping of the sample. Which party bears the cost of samples and shipping should be addressed in the manufacturing agreement with the factory.

It is important at this stage to communicate with the factory regarding your packaging specifications and labeling instructions. When a sample of the product and packaging is ready, you will review it with you for approval or modification. After a sample is approved, a final price is negotiated. You can then place your first production order.

Tooling Procurement

In order to manufacture products, your factory may need to procure tools to use in making components of the product, or the product itself. For example, many products contain plastic injection–molded pieces, which are made using a unique mold. The procurement of the necessary tooling for a product is a critical part of the product sourcing process.

Lower tooling costs are a major incentive for a company to manufacture its product offshore since tooling often involves substantial capital investment. In our experience, cost savings associated with using tools made by offshore manufacturers typically range from 35% to 50%. Moreover, many factories are willing to share the costs of such tools with their customer or amortize the cost of tooling over an agreed-upon volume of products purchased. This combination of lower cost, many factories' willingness to share this cost, and the opportunity to amortize the cost of tooling over an agreed-upon level of production offer substantial capital savings for your business.

The development of tooling obviously is one of the most fundamental aspects of sourcing a product. Without tools, you can't make the product. It also can be time consuming, as making molds or other tools can take up to sixty days or more. It's critical to consider both the cost and the time required for tooling in developing a timeline to bring product to market.

Fortunately, over the years, technology has improved the accuracy and shortened the timeline for producing quality tools. Most factories utilize tooling subcontractors who, in turn, utilize CAD systems to develop tools. This allows for 3D tool drawing to be shared in near real time during the development process. Adjustments can be made before the initial mold is cut, resulting in both cost and time savings.

In addition, 3D-printed samples allow customers to review an actual sample of a product before the tool is created. This reduces errors in the tool-making process and can avoid the need for tool revisions. 3D samples can offer dramatic cost and time savings in the tooling development process.

Product Commercialization

Commercializing a product is a process of converting a design into a product that can be both manufactured and shipped to meet a commercially viable price point. From a manufacturing perspective, this involves reviewing each step of the manufacturing process to minimize materials and labor usage and improving overall production efficiency. To achieve these goals, materials may be substituted, machinery may be utilized to reduce labor costs, and the organization of materials procurement and assembly line layout must all be carefully considered. The commercialization process often involves compromise and tradeoffs in order to deliver a commercially viable product.

Another key factor in the commercialization of a product is packaging products to maximize shipping efficiency. This involves things like tweaking the shape of products to allow them to "nest" more efficiently within a box, considering whether to palletize the product for shipment versus floor loading, and the like. Each of these decisions can have incremental effects on the landed cost of your product, and often the difference between a modest success and a profitable "home run."

Production Management

Critical to the effective production management is the establishment of regular reporting to the factory. For example, you should know what materials are ordered, when they will arrive at the factory, when your order is scheduled to begin production, when it will complete production, and when it is scheduled for shipment. Depending on your product, it may be advisable to closely track the procurement by your factory of key materials, so that problems can be identified early on and adjustments are made if necessary. By establishing quality reporting, you will have greater visibility into your supply chain, allowing you to make necessary adjustments, including re-allocating production to alternative factory, if things hit a snag.

Another key aspect of an efficient supply chain is production management. This requires a transparent relationship with your factory that allows you to understand each step of the production process and visibility into materials procurement and production lead times.

Quality Control

One of the largest challenges in sourcing a product is ensuring its quality. Based on our experience over the past 18 years, we consistently focus on the quality drivers, discussed in Chapter 2.

On-Time Delivery

The cost effective and timely delivery of your orders is a critical aspect of supply chain efficiency. As we have reviewed in this chapter, timely delivery of your order is a function of multiple factors. This includes the beginning of a well-thought-out design, careful focus in the product development process, selection of a quality factory, management of tooling procurement, the product sampling process on timely basis, prompt commercialization of the product, production management, and buttoned-down quality control procedures. However, successfully running the gauntlet represented by those elements of the sourcing process will not in and of itself often ensure timely delivery of your orders. In other words, in addition to efficient manufacturing of your product, careful attention must also be paid to the most rapid and cost-effective shipping route and modes.

Coordination of timely pickup of your order from the factory, shipment of the order by a rapid and cost-effective route, proficiently clearing customs, and coordination of inland transportation to the final destination are all key elements of a just-in-time delivery and an efficient supply chain. In addition, as noted above, careful attention should be paid to maximizing shipping efficiency (the number of products per container) and ease of loading and unloading the containers. This includes advice on how to best utilize container space and how to better package your products to withstand shipment in harsh weather conditions. In addition, it's helpful to have experience with shipping routes in relation with port authorities and leading freight forwarders, as this can make a huge difference to challenges that arise.

While most businesses generally prefer cost of ocean shipment, air shipment are sometimes the only way to meet urgent delivery deadlines. Before arranging shipment, care should be taken to evaluate whether the order delivery time actually makes sense in light of the higher delivery cost.

A consideration in shipping your products is opportunities that may exist to consolidate orders from multiple factories at one location prior to shipment to the country of origin. Consolidated shipments reduce shipping costs and often allow you to enhance inventory terms.

Case Study: Horseshoes!

In 2018 we were hired by an elite brand of shoes for horses. Unlike traditional, U-shaped, iron horseshoes, our client's shoes actually slipped onto the horse's hoof and were used to improve grip for certain types of riding. In addition, it had a line of horseshoes for veterinary use.

At the time they hired us, the client had an antiquated supply chain characterized by a lack of transparency and higher costs, and it didn't own unique tools used to produce its product. Our mission on its behalf was to re-source its existing products and work with it to develop a new generation of products. In doing so, our goals were to create a transparent, lower-cost supply chain, ensure ownership of unique production tools by our client, and mitigate supply chain risk. Regarding supply chain risk, the client was particularly motivated to transition its production out of China, where its products had become subject to so-called "Trump Tariffs."

Our work on behalf of this client was complicated by its absence of detailed product specifications or drawings. Therefore, our initial work involved translating prototypes created by its entrepreneur into detailed drawings and a bill of materials. Our team worked closely with the factory to develop detailed drawings and material specifications for each of the client's existing products as well as its new generation of products.

Fundamental to the product development process was educating the factories about the dramatic differences between horseshoes and shoes worn by humans. Obviously, the weight of the horse is dramatically greater than that of a human, and the stress placed on a shoe by the horse while riding full gallop is dramatically more than generated by even the most accomplished and professional human athlete. This required careful analysis of all key product materials. And, candidly, the commercialization of many of these products involved considerable trial and error.

The sampling process for these products was also extensive, as products that look good and withstand considerable stress applied by a human would not survive even the lightest use by a horse and rider.

Therefore, the sampling process for the product took considerable time, as our client would literally test them on rides that lasted many miles and were conducted under varying weather conditions. Nonetheless, over time, samples reached a quality standard that matched the customer's requirement.

Along the way, we worked closely with our factory to develop injection-molding tools for unique components of the products. To do this, we needed to aggregate a sufficient amount of business with each factory to ensure its management believed that an investment in the tooling owned by our client but initially paid for by the factory was a good investment. Also, we took care to ensure that all unique production tooling was owned by our client.

Once we had a functional product, we worked closely to improve its manufacturing during the commercialization process. We also made adjustments to ensure that all rough edges and other aspects of the products that might injure the horse were carefully modified. Once the samples were finalized, we developed a detailed quality control checklist based on our learning during the product development process. For example, we used tensile strength and other tests to ensure the performance of every component in the product.

As a result of our efforts, the client achieved all of its supply chain goals: it re-sourced its existing products to lower-cost factories in Vietnam, thereby avoiding Trump Tariffs on all new purchases and realizing overall product savings in excess of 40%. Its new generation of products also were brought to market on a timely basis. Perhaps most importantly, it established a transparent relationship with its factories that offered a true first cost for the product and gained ownership of its production tools in the process.

| 4 |

RELATIONSHIPS

"Do unto others as you would have them do unto you."
—Jesus of Nazareth

A successful global supply chain involves important relational investments, typically across culture, language, and unfamiliar business practices. In our experience, companies that build efficient supply chains tend to enjoy people and cross-cultural relationships. This requires effort but is not rocket science. By investing in key relationships, trust is built. This enhances transparency and the ability to manage any problems as they arise. In this chapter, we share a few guidelines on how to develop lasting, mutually beneficial relationships.

The Golden Rule

In business, your personal life, or across cultures or generations, those who adhere to the Golden Rule are successful in relationships.

While the Golden Rule is not difficult to understand, it is difficult to live by, especially if one's paradigm is that business is a zero-sum game, or the other person must lose in order for you to win. Companies that realize efficient global supply chains typically understand the value of a long-term partnership. They desire their suppliers and each player in their supply chains to be successful, just as they hope to be. Sadly, many fail to grasp this approach. Common mistakes I've observed over the years in a business communicating with its factory include the following:

- Over-representation of volume of products you will purchase. Businesses are accustomed to realizing a price discount if they place large orders, it's common for a business to maturely over-state its annual order quantity. The expectation is that this will be motivating for the factory and result in the factory quoting a lower price for the product. Of course, once the relationship begins, the factory will be able to observe firsthand that it was misled and the level of trust between the business and the factory will be diminished. Trust is a key currency in international trade, and once lost, it is difficult to reclaim. This is a classic scenario where the effort to realize a short-term gain will likely result in the long-term adverse consequences.

- Another common mistake in relating with a factory is to aggressively communicate that you have alternative suppliers. My observation is that many businesses do this to "keep the factory on its toes" but the effect is often the opposite. Such comments tend to demotivate a factory, underscore that the investment required to take on production of your product is risky since you communicated that you may take your production elsewhere. I think it's fair to understand that your factory, like you, is well aware that it operates in a competitive marketplace and that you have other manufacturing options.

Spend Time Getting to Know your Partners

One of the surest ways to build a relationship is to communicate interest in your supply chain partners and allow them to get to know you. Just as you would with any friendship, focus on getting to know the owners or key management of your factories and key supply chain partners. They will appreciate your interest, and likewise, they will want to know you. International business is characterized by a certain mystique—a lack of knowledge about your counterparty. By allowing your partners to know you, and communicating interest in their lives, you will naturally win them over, and you and your projects will become a priority to them.

To know and be known, of course, requires regular contact. Make it a priority to visit them at their factory location, spend time with them over dinner and on activities they enjoy. In addition, welcome them to visit you and share your interests with them.

The investments you make over time on your relationships with your factory owners and key management is like depositing money in the bank. One day you will need it! The effort taken to create a reserve will bear fruit at a time when others, who have failed to make a relationship are unable to execute.

Successful relationships must be created face-to-face, not online. No amount of WeChat messages, social media posts, and the like can substitute for the conversations about shared values, including family life, the role of doing business, and the like.

Treating your factory partner as you would have yourself treated and spending time getting to know them are not just nice things to do. They are also prudent business tactics. Over the years, we have repeatedly experienced the good fruit of investing relationally with our supply chain partners. Some examples of this include:

- A factory owner traveled to the United States to support a business in its meeting with a key customer. This support by the owner gave the customer confidence that the factory was committed to supporting rapid growth and demand for the product.
- In order to meet seasonal demands that required urgent delivery, a factory delayed departure by its workers for a national holiday to ensure timely completion of our client's orders.
- On its own initiative, a factory developed a significant innovation for one of our client's products, saving the client cost and allowing it to further differentiate itself from its competitors.

- During the COVID-19 pandemic, the workers at the factory had to live in a "bubble" at the factory to ensure that orders were timely produced. The workers had gone home to be with their family, the "bubble" had been burst and the factory would have been forced to shut down.

Given the strong relationships we encourage with our factories, it is common for factories to offer increasingly generous payment terms over time. This benefits our clients' cash flow and typically allows them to grow faster. Future growth, in turn, leads to larger orders for the factory.

As these examples illustrate, treating others well and taking an interest in their lives is simply good business. By investing in the relationship with another, you are literally placing "money in bank" that will be available when you need to draw upon it in the future. Therefore, another way to think of how you engage your factory has a direct bearing on your ability to manage supply chain risk.

In my experience, very few businesses make an effort to express gratitude to their factory sources. As human beings, we all appreciate when someone thanks us for our effort, and this is no less true in the context of international trade. Over the years, I've made it standard operating procedure to thank each factory I interact with for their support to our client. The factory management often seems surprised to be thanked, that our gratitude does not go unnoticed, and directly benefits our clients.

Relationships matter in business. We are all relational, and we're motivated to do our best for those who treat us well, express interest in our lives, and communicate gratitude for a job well done. This is a simple human nature.

In the context of international trade, relationships are even more important, because trust is key to overcome the inherent mistrust and risk of a global supply chain. I can't begin to tell you how many problems we've been able to resolve over the years on the simple basis that our partner trusted us to keep our word without taking advantage of them. Stated in another way, trust is the currency that allows the resolution of many challenges and offers the ability to keep your supply chain operating smoothly when those of your competitor's fail.

Case Study: Nursery and Gardening Products

In 2006 a start-up manufacturer of commercial nursery industry and indoor gardening products hired us to assist it. Its products included plastic propagation containers, flowerpots, and growing containers made of a felt-like material. While the products were simple, the technology used by our client resulted in plants with a superior root system.

The market for their products was very price competitive. Moreover, meeting their challenging price requirements required the use of low-cost, recycled materials. This, in turn, dramatically raised the risk of product defects, as maintaining consistent performance of the recycled plastic used in their products was challenging. In addition, because the client's products used proprietary technologies, it was critical to establish protection over their intellectual property from the outset.

Over the past 16 years, our client's director of development has worked hard to develop mutually beneficial relationships with his factories. In the early stages of the relationship, our client worked hard to educate the factories, providing valuable context for the "why" in his products. He effectively shared his company's vision and how its products fit into the market. He also took an interest in each factory's business apart from his company's needs in an effort to understand how he might better cooperate to meet their needs.

Early visits were characterized by him providing gifts that had meaning in his own life and allowed the clients to better understand his background and values. Over the many years since establishing his factory relationships, the client has hosted the owners of the Chinese factories at his home in the United States and involved them with his friends.

Also, some of his unique product requirements helped the factories to develop skills that allowed them to make plastic pots for other customers that sold to markets other than those protected for our client in his contracts with each factory. Naturally, the factories were grateful for their success with these alternative products and attributed their success to product knowledge acquired from our client.

Over time, the friendship between our client and his factory bore great fruit. Our client's factories now allow him to place orders without making any deposits. Moreover, his factories have extended his company payment terms of 45 days from the date products are shipped. In addition, after our client lost a major customer, he and his factories worked closely to establish even longer payment terms, which allows our client to manage a difficult business transition.

Over the past 16 years, our client has worked hard to develop close relationships with his company's suppliers. He has enjoyed travel to Asia and the friendships established along the way. While his interest in relating with his factory is driven by a genuine desire for friendship, it has also obviously paid huge business dividends.

| 5 |

DO CONTRACTS MATTER?

"Good paper makes good friends." —Anonymous

As revealed in the old adage above, contracts can create a framework in which relationships can prosper. This is certainly true in the product sourcing relationship between your business and its factory. Yet many business owners rush into trade relationships without preparing proper paperwork. The results can be disastrous. In our experience, the main purpose of a well-drafted manufacturing agreement is not to manage a factory by threat of litigation. Assuming a buyer has followed the product process described in Chapter 3, challenges with a manufacturer will likely be discovered early. As a result, it's likely that damages will be modest, and a business resolution to the problem will be achieved. In over 26 years, none of our clients have experienced a loss that warranted litigation.

Nonetheless, well-drafted contracts help define expectations and the roles and responsibilities of the parties. As such, they are valued tools for establishing a win-win relationship with your supplier.

In my experience, going over a well-drafted contract with your supplier is a critical exercise. This is because a well-drafted contract will address the fundamentals of a sourcing relationship described in Chapter 2: price, quality, delivery, and risk management. A well-drafted contract will also define the sourcing process step-by-step. Reviewing a contract with your factory early on in your relationship will help identify potential problem areas and allow the parties to proactively address them. In addition, the mere existence of a contract communicates to the factory the seriousness with which you view the relationship.

Apart from defining a relationship with the factory relative to manufacture of the product, a good manufacturing agreement will also address key elements of your overall supply chain efficiency. For example, it may require you to provide production forecasts, which allows the company to preorder material. This, in turn, will result in lower product prices and shorten production lead time, since the factory will have prepurchased material required for your production. Moreover, a good contract will establish your rights to inspect the materials, oversee production process, and conduct quality control inspections prior to shipment. It also should provide you with recourse if product defects are discovered after your product ships. In addition, it will define payment terms, define when title to your products transfers, allocate risk of loss, and address coordination of shipments once the production is complete.

Viewed in this manner, a well-drafted manufacturing agreement is essentially a road map that will guide not only your relationship with the factory but inform key deliverables affecting the overall efficiency of your supply chain as well.

As we will see in Chapter 6, your contract with your factory is also a good way to promote social compliance in your manufacturing relationship.

In our experience, you should have at least two contracts in place with your factory source. First, before ensuring detailed product information with the factory, you should enter into a nondisclosure, noncompetition, non-circumvention ("NNN") agreement. This will protect you against an unscrupulous factory using your information to compete against you or in selling directly to your customers. A reputable company will sign an NNN agreement as a matter of course.

In addition to an NNN agreement, prior to having a manufacturer make samples for you, you should have in place a manufacturing agreement. And if your product is branded, the manufacturing agreement should include an intellectual property license covering applicable trademarks, copyrights, and patents. As a matter of best practice, your standard NNN agreement and manufacturing agreement should be bilingual but specify that the governing language is English. Likewise, the agreements should dictate the applicable law and a dispute resolution process that would allow you to obtain and enforce a judgement against the factory if it breached contract.

| 6 |

SOCIAL COMPLIANCE

"Corporate Social Responsibility is a hard-edged business decision. Not because it is a nice thing to do or because people are forcing us to do it but because it is good for our business." —Niall FitzGerald, former chairman and CEO of Unilever

In response to media coverage of child labor, sweatshop conditions, human trafficking, and environmental degradation associated with offshore, lower-cost manufacturing, there is a growing movement to ensure that factories are socially compliant. This movement is driven by humanitarian organizations, labor unions (who view social compliance is a means of protecting domestic jobs), and environmental organizations (who desire to leverage consumer purchasing power pressure and environmental compliance to the manufacturing process).

Although many American companies that manufactured products in a manner that failed to meet social compliance standards, much of the media attention on the subject focused on Nike. Nike, in response, adopted extensive social compliance programs and addressed management in governance issues to ensure those standards were implemented. While social standards are far reaching, the principal focus is in the following areas:

- <u>Child Labor.</u> Many industries adopted laws prohibiting child labor in the 19th century. These requirements can be extended through the contract manufacturing process to any factory.
- <u>Payment of Prevailing Wages.</u> Many Western countries adopted minimum wage laws in the 20th century. It is now common that manufacturing agreements include requirements that the factory sources pay prevailing wages for the area in which the factory is located.
- <u>Worker's Safety.</u> Many Western countries also adopted or placed safety requirements to protect workers against danger common to the manufacturing process. Many of these same standards are extended by contact to factory sources.
- <u>Forced Labor.</u> Sadly, many countries either support or overlook the use of forced labor. This is another area of social compliance addressed by many businesses in the factory selection or manufacturing agreement process.
- <u>Human Trafficking.</u> In recent years, there is an increasing awareness on the part of Western consumers of human trafficking. In some cases, human trafficking is part and parcel to forced labor and is again addressed in the factory selection and contracting process. In addition, as noted below, increasingly the US manufacturers are required to disclose measures they have taken to combat human trafficking in their supply chain.
- <u>Environmental Protection.</u> It is well known that many low-cost manufacturing operations border on environmental protections, if protections even exist in the countries in which they operate. Increasingly, Western consumers desire to know that the products they purchase are manufactured using environmentally compliant standards.

The need for businesses to offshore manufacturing in a manner that is socially compliant is a growing trend. Its immediate relevance to businesses, however, is driven by applicable laws and the environment to which a business sells its product.

The California Transparency and Supply Chains Act, for example, requires businesses to post the measures they have taken to address human trafficking in their supply chain in a prominent position on their website. The act is intended to fight slavery and human trafficking by requiring retail sellers and manufacturers to disclose on their corporate website the specific measures taken to eradicate slavery and human trafficking. It requires the California Franchise Tax Board to make available to the California attorney general each year a list of retailers and manufacturers required to make such disclosures and grants the attorney general authority to enforce the law against companies who fail to comply. Perhaps even more threatening for a noncomplying business, the act makes it easier for the consumers to damage a company's brand or reputation, alleging noncompliance.

Another example of the United States law aimed at social compliance is Proposition 65. Proposition 65 requires businesses to provide warning to consumers about significant exposures to chemicals that cause cancer, birth defects, or other reproductive disorders. This list, which must be updated at least once a year, has grown to include over 800 chemicals since it was first published in the 1987. Proposition 65 requires businesses to notify Californians about significant amounts of chemicals in the products they purchase, in their homes or workplaces, or that are released into the environment. The intention of this is to enable people to make informed decisions about protecting themselves from exposure to these chemicals.

Since Proposition 65 is focused on protecting Californians, many foreign suppliers have not had a reason to comply with it. Therefore, in order to sell products in California, confirming that materials used in a product are Proposition 65 compliant might be a significant challenge for your business.

In addition to the laws that protect social compliance, the preferences of a business's customers also play an important role. For example, if your product is sold into a labor union environment, you likely will want to be sensitive to ensure it is made in a socially compliant manner. By way of example, a few years ago we represented a manufacturer of hangers that were sold to a uniform company, which delivered a large percentage of its uniforms to companies with unionized labor forces. To avoid union pushback against hangers manufactured by workers in substandard working conditions, we worked with our client to engage a third-party social compliance auditor (see below) to audit and certify the social compliance of its factory. That audit resulted in the factory adopting numerous new policies, including the provision of uniforms for all its employees, containing a minimum wage for its employees rather than compensating them on an individual performance and adopting measures to protect the environment from runoff from the paint booth where it painted its hangers. Based on certification of social compliance issued by the third-party auditor, the client was able to sell hangers to the uniform company without pushback from the company's unionized workers.

Another driver of social compliance is the preferences of end user consumers. Many consumers are motivated to purchase a product if they know that it was manufactured in a socially compliant manner.

Many businesses, in an effort to demonstrate their commitment to manufacturing in a socially compliant way, seek certification of their practices. An example would be to have your products fair-trade certified. This requires your business to satisfy a series of standards applicable to your industry and allows your product to be branded as fair-trade certified.

To address social compliance concerns in the manufacturing of your product, we recommend that you take the following actions:

- Arrange for an audit of the factories you are considering for sourcing a product. The audit should include a visit by someone on your team or an independent third party and address specific measures the factory takes: avoid child labor, payment of prevailing wages, ensure safe working conditions, prohibit forced labor and human trafficking, and protect the environment. In our experience, quality factories already have these policies in place or are willing to adopt them to obtain your business.

- Secondly, your manufacturing agreement with factory should include social compliance standards important to you, your customers, and other stakeholders. While you cannot enforce provisions on a daily basis, communicating them clearly to the factory as part of the contract review demonstrates your seriousness of compliance.

- Third, as noted with the hanger manufacturer example above, it may be prudent to engage a third party to conduct an audit of the factory and certify its compliance with relevant aspects of social compliance.

In my experience, quality manufacturers care about their employees and desire to be good corporate citizens. But they likely will not understand your values and social compliance standards unless you communicate them clearly, reinforcing that you view compliance with social standards are critical to the success of your relationship with the factory. It's important to communicate these expectations from the very outset of your relationship with your factory.

Case Study: Hanger Supplier

In 2009, we were hired by a supplier of wire hangers to a nationally known business uniform company. The uniform company delivered uniforms to its corporate customers on the wire hangers supplied by our client. At the time, the United States had imposed punitive tariffs on the importation of wire hangers from China, and our client was looking for a factory source other than in China. In addition, because many of the uniforms were delivered to companies with union shops, our client needed us to find a factory that met social compliance criteria in order to avoid creating a problem for the business to which the uniforms were supplied.

Within a few weeks, we had identified an alternative manufacturing source for wire hangers in Vietnam. However, our visit to the factory revealed a variety of social compliance concerns, particularly in the area of environmental protection. For example, many of the wire hangers were painted in a paint booth that discharged used paint into a nearby stream. Not only was this environmentally damaging, but it also involved excessive waste.

There were also employee health concerns. For example, some of the hangers required the application of glue to cardboard tube to prevent pants from sliding off the hanger. Our factory visit revealed that the glue was applied in areas of the factory that were not well ventilated—and that many of the workers in this area were women of child-bearing age.

In order to ensure that our client met social compliance standards required by its customers, we hired a third-party social compliance auditing firm to visit the factory and recommend appropriate changes. As a result, factory workers wages were restructured; all factory employees were provided with fresh uniforms and upgraded working conditions. Paint booths were installed to ensure that overspray was properly collected and disposed of and ventilation in areas where glue was applied to so-called "strut" hangers was dramatically improved and women of child-bearing age were assigned to other roles in the production process.

Throughout the process, the factory leadership was cooperative, viewing the audit as a means of improving their production processes and employee relations. Also, they knew that meeting social compliance criteria was critical to earning our client's business and trust.

Once all the social compliance changes were adopted and production began, our client realized significant savings relative to its cost of manufacturing wire hangers in China. And, of course, it saved the cost of the tariffs applicable to wire hangers imported from China. Moreover, customers could represent to their unions that the hangers were manufactured in a manner that did not disadvantage American workers.

| 7 |

PAYMENT TERMS

"If you think nobody cares about you, try missing a couple of payments." —Steve Wright

The payment terms you negotiate with your factory source have dramatic implications for your company's capital requirements and growth potential. Payment terms are inherently a matter between the seller and the buyer, so careful attention to developing a relationship with your factory is key to the achievement of favorable terms (*see* Chapter 4 above).

In addition to having a relationship with your factory, payment terms are dictated by a variety of other factors. One such factor is current market conditions. For example, during the COVID-19 pandemic, manufacturers of personal protective equipment enjoyed an uber seller's market that allowed them to demand advance payment before they would even accept an order for production! Stated another way, whether your factory needs your business is a key consideration in whether it will offer attractive payment terms.

Another obvious consideration affecting a factory's willingness to offer payment terms is its own financial strength. If it is undercapitalized, it may need some amount of prepayment in order to purchase materials necessary for your production. On the other hand, if the factory is well financed, it may see value in using its financial strength to essentially subsidize your production, with the intent of promoting growth of your business and making you more dependent on it as a factory source.

A third factor that affects payment terms is your understanding of the factory's needs. For example, your willingness to provide production forecast allows the factory to more efficiently manage materials procurement and production. This, in turn, makes it more likely to cooperate with your payment needs.

Perhaps the greatest determining factor in relating to payment terms is length of relationship. Initially, most factories are hesitant to grant payment terms as they have not yet experienced timely payment. As time goes by, however, if you consistently and timely pay your factory, your factory's willingness to take a risk on not being paid for goods produced increases. Therefore, it is common that your payment terms will improve with time.

On the other hand, if payment issues arrive, it is not uncommon that a factory will seek to renegotiate payment terms to make them less favorable.

Like any relationship, success is often the result of adversity. Most factory owners will understand if your business hits a bump in the road. But it will be critical for you to communicate the challenges you are facing to your factory and give them a payment plan that you can satisfy. Overcoming a rough patch can actually lead to a stronger relationship and improved payment terms if properly managed.

While every factory is different, it is common that a relationship begins with the following payment terms: 30% deposit with your order, and with the balance due prior to shipment. There are of course variations to these terms, depending upon the factory's interest in the product, perception of your financial strength, etc. Nonetheless, this tends to be the starting point for payment terms.

Another factor that can affect payment terms is the purchaser's ability to guarantee payment. For example, years ago, most production was secured by bank letters of credit. International standards applicable to such letters of credit made a factory confident that it would be paid for the products purchased. Moreover, a factory could often make draws against the letter of credit to purchase production materials. On the other hand, a letter of credit typically involves a business dedicating a portion of its credit facility to that purpose. Letters of credit also involve bank fees that raise business costs. Most businesses prefer to avoid this, as it decreases flexibility to access their credit facilities.

As international trade has expanded, businesses are increasingly willing to accept by means of wire transfer. This option, obviously, is much more flexible for the purchaser, which is why it has become the norm. When making wire transfers, however, a buyer should be aware that more than one factory can be tricked by a sophisticated fraudster, and wire money to the fraudster's account, rather than the factory. To address this risk, your business should have in place a strict protocol relating to wire payments to factories, particularly if the factory's bank wire instructions change.

As noted above, payment terms have a dramatic impact on use of your company's capital. Therefore, careful attention should be paid in selecting factories that are able to offer payment terms and in working with the factory to help it efficiently plan your production. This takes time, but it's well worth the effort.

In our experience, most clients start with payment terms requiring a deposit and final payment before shipment. Then, over time, the relationship evolves to include a factory that is premaking products to maximize manufacturing efficiency and reduce individual order's production lead times, shipping the product before being paid, and then providing terms of varying durations.

Case Study: Electric Scooter Distributor

As noted above in Chapter 4, investing in the relationship with your factory's owners can pay positive dividends in terms of enhanced trust and improved payment terms. Conversely, the failure to develop close factory relationships can have the opposite effect.

In 2021 we were hired by a distributor of electric scooters and unicycles. While our client had identified qualified suppliers of these products, travel restrictions related to the COVID-19 pandemic had prevented it from establishing strong relationships. Meanwhile, its business was growing at a dramatic pace, and the failure of its suppliers to support it with payment terms was suffocating its ability to grow.

The client's inability to secure favorable payment terms from its factories stretched its working capital to the breaking point, costing it millions of dollars in lost sales. Yet its factories, because they didn't feel trust with our client, refused to cooperate on payment terms.

Apart from relationships, another factor that affects a factory's willingness to provide payment terms is its own assessment of whether it needs to. This is a function of market conditions, the uniqueness of your product, and whether the factory believes it is necessary to support your growth. In the case of the electric scooter company, its factories assessed that demand was very strong and that our client couldn't easily get a better deal from an alternative supplier. Therefore, it took a non-relational, transactional approach to business.

As a result, despite the obvious need of our client for support from its factories, they refused to provide payment terms. This refusal, in our client's time of greatest need, did not go unnoticed. Over time, the client will undoubtedly choose factories that are more supportive of its growth objectives.

| 8 |

WHAT IF MY PRODUCT NEEDS TO BE "MADE-IN-AMERICA?"

"America is the worst country on earth – except for all the others." –Winston S. Churchill

Many businesses serve customers that require the products they purchase be "Made-in-America." Examples include some product sales to the US government or sales by a brand that desires to maintain a Made-in-America image. In addition, as noted in Chapter 6, sales of a product into a labor union environment often require sensitivity to Made-in-America sentiment.

Interestingly, the phrase Made-in-America virtually never means that the *entire* product, including all of its components, must be manufactured in the United States. For example, automobile fleets of the US auto brands (e.g. Ford and General Motors) contain only 50% domestic content on average. Yet these cars can be marketed to the consumer as "American Made."

Likewise, federal and military acquisition regulations have unique rules that allow almost 50% of the value of a Made-in-America product to be made overseas. In addition, if a product that is not generally available from a domestic source, exceptions to Made-in-America requirements may apply.

In determining whether your product satisfies Made-in-America requirements, you will need to pay close attention to the specific requirements of your customer. However, it's likely that your customer's specific needs will more or less track the following legal standards for Made-in-America products that have evolved over time.

All or Virtually All Standard

There is no law that requires most products sold in the US to be marked or labeled Made in USA (with the exception of automobiles, textile, wool, and fur products[2]). However, manufacturers who choose to mark the US content of their products must comply with the Federal Trade Commission Made in USA policy.[3]

For a product to be called Made in USA or claimed to be of domestic origin without qualification or limits on the claim, the product must be "all or virtually all" made in the US. The term "United States," as referred to in the Enforcement Policy Statement, includes the 50 states, the District of Columbia, and the US territories and possessions.

"All or virtually all" means that all significant parts and processing that go into the product must be of the US origin. That is, the product should contain no, or negligible, foreign content. A manufacturer needs competent and reliable evidence to back up the claim that its product is "all or virtually all" made in the US.

In addition to the minimum threshold, discussed above, the Commission will consider other factors to determine if a product is of the US origin, including:

- The product's final assembly or processing must take place in the US
- How much of the product's total manufacturing cost can be assigned to the US parts and processing.

- How far removed any foreign content is from the finished product. In some instances, only a small portion of the total manufacturing costs are attributable to foreign processing, but that processing represents a significant amount of the product's overall processing.[4]

When analyzing the percentage of domestic content in a particular product, manufacturers should use the cost of goods sold or inventory costs of finished goods in their analysis. Such costs generally are limited to the total cost of all manufacturing materials, direct manufacturing labor, and manufacturing overhead. If given in good faith, manufacturers can rely on information from suppliers about the domestic content in the parts, components, and other elements they produce. However, manufacturers should ask suppliers for specific information about the percentage of US-origin content in elements.

To determine the percentage of US content, manufacturers should look back far enough in the manufacturing process to be reasonably sure that any significant foreign content has been included in their assessment of foreign costs. Foreign content incorporated early in the manufacturing process often will be less significant to consumers than the content that is a direct part of the finished product or the parts or components produced by the immediate supplier. Raw materials may be included in the evaluation of whether a product is "all or virtually all" made in the US depending on how much of the product's costs are from raw materials of US-origin and how far removed from the finished product they are.

Where the percentage of foreign content is de minimis or very low, it is more likely that the commission will consider the product "all or virtually all" made in the United States. There is no fixed point for this determination and the commission will conduct this inquiry on a case-by-case basis balancing the factors discussed above as well as the nature of the product and consumers' expectations to determine whether an enforcement action is warranted.[5]

Even if all of the parts of a final product are made in the US, it is a prerequisite that the product be "substantially transformed" in the United States in order to be considered Made in the USA. The substantial transformation test is discussed in further detail below.

Substantial Transformation

Articles that are substantially transformed or wholly manufactured in the United States are under the exclusive jurisdiction of the Federal Trade Commission ("FTC") labeling regulations under the Tariff Act of 1930.

Where an imported product incorporates materials or processing from more than one country, the country of origin is the last country in which a "substantial transformation" took place. Pursuant to 19 CFR 134.35:

An article used in the United States in manufacture which results in an article having a name, character, or use differing form that of the imported article, will be within the principle of that decision in the case of United States v. Gibson-Thomsen Co., Inc., 27 C.C.P.A. 267 (C.A.D. 98). Under this principle, the manufacturer or processor in the United States who converts or combines the imported article into the different article will be considered the "ultimate purchaser" of the imported article within the contemplation of section 304(a), Tariff Act of 1930, as amended (19 USC. 1304(a)), and the article shall be excepted from marking.[6]

Under the Gibson-Thompson test, "a product undergoes a 'substantial transformation' if, as a result of further manufacturing or processing, the product loses its identity and is transformed into a new product having a new name, character [,] and use."[7] The FTC explains in its policy statement that,

A substantial transformation is a manufacturing or other process that results in a new and different article of commerce, having a new name, character and use that is different from that which existed prior to the processing. Country-of-origin determinations using the substantial transformation test are made on a case-by-case basis through administrative determinations by the Customs Service.[8]

For example, a bottle that is filled retains a separate character, from its contents and is not substantially transformed into a new product. By contrast, the bristles of a toothbrush, when combined with other items, are transformed to become a toothbrush.[9]

Though a product entering the US that will be "substantially transformed" does not need a country of origin marking, the outermost container that carries the imported articles must be marked.[10]

Value Test

The Buy American Act (the "BAA") grants preferential pricing advantage to government contractors through a price evaluation penalty applied to competing offers of foreign products. To be considered a domestic end product for government procurement purposes, the BAA requires that the product be both:

1. manufactured in the US; and
2. contains more than fifty percent US component parts.[11]

There is no definition for "manufactured" under the BAA. "Component" is defined as "an article, material, or supply incorporated directly into an end product."[12]

Even if a product qualifies as a domestic end product pursuant to the BAA, it does not follow that it can be labeled "Made-in-America." In order to be labeled as such, it still must satisfy the FTC's "all or virtually all" standard, discussed above.

As you can see, the fact that your customer desires a Made-in-America product does not necessarily mean the product must be made in its entirety in the United States. Multiple strategies exist to qualify your product as Made-in-America product. One such strategy involves combining imported and domestically sourced components into a final product in which the value of imported components are less than 50% of the total value of the final product.

Another strategy involves the importation of raw materials, which are then "substantially transformed" into the product you ultimately sell to your customer.

In summary, don't be deterred by your customer's requirement that it be Made-in-America. Instead, think outside the box, keeping in mind that most buyers of Made-in-America products expect to pay a higher price.

The United States-Mexico-Canada Free Trade Agreement offers another means of qualifying your product as "Made-in-America." Under the USMCA, products made either in Canada or Mexico qualify as "Made-in-America" for purposes of federal procurement regulations. Particularly for a product made in Mexico, which in turn may be manufactured using component from other foreign countries, this exception can offer meaningful Made-in-America marketing opportunities for your product.

As you can see, it is important to understand that the requirement that a product be Made-in-America does not necessarily require that the *entirety* of the product be made in the United States. Instead, the Made-in-America requirement should be a signal for you to take a deeper dive into what is actually meant by the Made-in-America requirement of your customer.

Case Study: Laser Gunsite Manufacturer

In 2008, we were hired by a manufacturer of laser gunsites. Its gunsites were highly sought after by the US military, as their green laser beams offered a visible means of communicating danger to the enemy during the Iraq War. US soldiers at a checkpoint could simply place a green laser beam on an approaching target as means of maintaining control at critical checkpoints.

US military regulations require that most procured products be "Made-in-America." But our client's gunsites were manufactured in Taiwan. The client sought our advice on what it might do to satisfy

US military procurement regulations. Otherwise, it was at risk of losing the largest market for its product.

After several meetings with our client, we suggested they re-package this laser gunsite "product" by combining the laser gunsite with a domestically made "Molle Pouch," which would allow the gunsite to be carried efficiently as part of a soldier's uniform. We also recommended that the client assemble the Taiwanese-made laser and the domestically made Molle Pouch components at a facility in the United States. In short, by combining the laser gunsite with a US-made Molle Pouch, the client was able to create a new, "Made-in-USA" product.

This was possible because the value of US manufactured components in the overall product exceeded the value of the laser gunsite made in Taiwan. Therefore, our client could, based on the value test, market its product to the US military as a "Made-in-America" product.

This resulted in our client gaining a large contract for its laser gun-sites. In addition, because the overall value of the product it was selling to the US military increased and it made the same percentage profit on each item sold, its total profits to supply gunsites to the military more than doubled!

| 9 |

HOW TO MANAGE TARIFFS ON MY PRODUCTS?

"Necessity is the mother of invention." —Derived from Plato's Republic

Until the Trump Administration, the general direction of international trade policy following World War II was to reduce tariffs. Consensus amongst economists and policy makers was that encouraging global trade served the common good, offering better quality products, reducing product costs, lifting people out of poverty, and creating an economic interdependence that serves as a deterrent to war. Like free enterprise generally, however, international trade created winners and losers, with losers typified by factory closures and lost jobs. These were particularly focused in the manufacturing regions of the United States and Europe, where unskilled workers saw their jobs exported to lower wage competitors in developing countries.

In response to the legitimate pain experienced by manufacturing workers who lost their jobs, the Trump Administration imposed tariffs on China, both to protect American jobs and as punishment for

China skirting rules intended to ensure a level playing field in the realm of international trade.

The Trump Tariffs, which combined with existing tariffs could impose aggregate import duties of over 30%, created severe pain for businesses who had become reliant upon foreign suppliers. Almost overnight their profit margins evaporated. This resulted in businesses employing a number of strategies to avoid tariffs. Some of these legitimate, but others violated the law. This Chapter addresses several of the more common strategies utilized by businesses to manage tariff risk.

Relocate Production to a Low-Tariff Country

As noted in the risk management section of Chapter 2, imposition of high tariffs injected in a new risk to international trade. For the previous 70 years, trade barriers had been declining, but now, suddenly, they dramatically increased. By and large this increase was focused on a single country, China. With the tariffs, China in many cases was no longer a low-cost supplier of products. And the heightened rhetoric between political leaders in the United States and China drew into question whether China would continue to be a low-risk supplier of products.

In response to higher costs and political uncertainty, businesses naturally looked for alternatives to manufacturing in China. Vietnam, for example, has experienced dramatic growth in its economy since the imposition of tariffs on China during the Trump Administration. Likewise, other Southeastern Asian countries and producers closer to North America (e.g. Guatemala, Mexico) have seen rapid increases in manufacturing activities as businesses have looked for alternative manufacturing to China. As noted in Chapter 2, when establishing a supply chain, it is critical to manage political risk. Manufacturers who have established alternative supply chain suppliers outside of China prior to imposition of the tariffs as means to manage risk were able to quickly shift production from China to factory sources in other countries quickly, avoiding the worst impacts of the tariffs. For business that were flatter footed, while shifting production from China still made economic sense, the transition took time.

Product Price Renegotiation

Another common strategy for businesses to manage tariff risk involved renegotiation of pricing with their factories. This typically involved some sort of tariff sharing between the factory and its customer with the factory willing to absorb a portion of the higher landed cost faced due to the new tariffs. In many cases, it was worth it to a factory to lower its prices (at least for the short term) to avoid losing the customer's business to alternative suppliers in other countries.

Your Factory Relocates Production to Another Country

In many cases, we observed that a Chinese factory was willing to establish a new manufacturing facility in a new, lower tariff country. For example, after the Trump Tariffs were imposed, many Chinese factories opened new factories in Vietnam or other Southeastern Asian countries as a strategy to avoid the tariffs.

Reallocation of Purchase Price between Product and Other Forms of Payment

Another strategy utilized by many businesses, particularly those that distributed a branded product made in China, involved re-allocation of the product price between the goods purchased and other form of payments (such as license fees) that are not subject to tariffs. Under this strategy, the factory receives the same amount of compensation for the products it produced, but a portion of the compensation was shifted from the product (which is subject to tariffs) to license fees (which were not subject to tariffs).

This strategy is not *per se* illegal; it must be supported by applicable facts and circumstances. For example, if the factory had charged $100 of product prior to impositions of tariffs and then immediately shifted to a pricing structure involving $70 product cost and a $30 license fee, the transaction obviously would appear to involve the evasion of tariffs by the US customer.

The second consideration involves scrutiny with regards to the legitimacy or amount of the license fee itself. In the example just given, government authorities would surely question whether a license fee of 30% reflected market rates.

A business found guilty of sham tariff shifting is subject to severe financial and criminal penalties. Moreover, the business could be barred from importing products in the future. Not only are financial and criminal penalties a deterrent to tariff shifting practices, but the corresponding businesses reputation can be devastating.

While tariff shifting practices were regularly used by importers or suppliers in response to Trump Tariffs, they should only be undertaken after a clear-eyed review of the relevant facts and circumstances and keen awareness of the consequence that can apply if the arrangement is scrutinized by government authorities.

Shipments from an Alternate Country of Origin

Another practice employed by many businesses and their factories to avoid high tariff involves the reshipment of substantially completed products made in China from an alternative country. For example, I experienced firsthand the practice of a competitor, who reshipped from Vietnam wire hangers manufactured in China. Under this scheme, the manufacturer in China shipped hangers to Vietnam, where the hangers were removed from their boxes and then repackaged in boxes indicating the product was made in Vietnam. This practice is illegal, as it violates the Country of Origin rules. The competitor involved suffered severe sanctions imposed by US Customs, including monetary fines and criminal sanctions.

While it is possible to ship a product from one country if it has components manufactured in another country, the importer and manufacturer must take care to comply with the relevant country of origin requirements. Those requirements are similar to Made-in-

America requirements discussed in Chapter 8. A summary of these requirements is set forth below.

US Customs and Border Protection and the Federal Trade Commission (FTC) have concurrent jurisdiction to require that foreign goods imported into the United States be marked with the country of origin. While Customs operates under the Tariff Act, which sets the conditions under with foreign goods may enter, the FTC has general power over all goods imported into and sold in the U.S under the Federal Trade Commission Act. Generally, the FTC regulates claims of US origin under its general authority to act against deceptive acts and practices,[13] while foreign-origin markings on articles are regulated by Customs[14].

The De Minimis Rule

Another practice employed by many businesses to avoid high tariffs involves the so-called De Minimis Rule. The intention of this rule is to allow American tourists to bring back souvenirs from overseas duty-free, but companies now use it to avoid billions of dollars in tariffs. The De Minimis Rule has been around for decades. Its name is derived from the Latin term meaning something too small to fuss with, and for many years, it was just that—accounting for such a small sliver of imports that US Customs and Border Protection didn't even bother to keep track of them.

However, all that has changed. US customs data show a sharp increase in number of De Minimis shipments in the wake of the Trump Administration's tariffs on Chinese goods, climbing from 299 million shipments in 2017 to 400 million shipments in 2018, the first year the tariff took effect. By 2021, the number had jumped to 1.71 billion shipments. The 2020 fiscal year, the US imported 618 billion dollars of consumer goods; experts estimate that the De Minimis shipment comprised over 10% of that value.

The growth of e-commerce and the imposition of high tariffs set forth by the Trump Administration has caused the amount of De Minimis imports to soar. The value of such imports into 2012 was approximately 40 million. By 2020, the value of De Minimis imports had soured to over 67 billion! Another factor contributing to growth in the value of De Minimis Rule imports was action taken by Congress in 2016 that raised the value of these imports to $800 up from $200. While multiple factors are at play, there can be no question that the De Minimis Rule is being used to avoid tariffs on an unprecedented scale.

Use of the De Minimis Rule to avoid tariffs is perfectly legal. It makes economic sense when the cost of shipping your product is less than the applicable tariff on the same product. The De Minimis Rule allows US retailers to sell foreign products (and foreign companies that sell directly to US consumers) to avoid tariffs on goods as long as they are packaged and addressed to individual buyers and fall below the $800 cap. As a result, many US retailers, particularly in the apparel sector, have shifted to a made-to-order strategy for their online, direct-to-consumer business, setting production runs based on actual customer orders. The goods, which are packaged and addressed to individual consumers, are then shipped directly from a foreign factory typically to a freight forwarder that bundles the shipments, and flies them to the US, where they are picked up by couriers for direct delivery to customers, skipping any warehousing or fulfillment in the US. For the US companies taking advantage of the De Minimis Rule in this manner, they typically are saving more on duties than extra amounts they pay for on shipping.

Tariff Act

Importation of Foreign Articles for Sale in the United States:

The Tariff Act regulates all foreign made articles imported into the United States for sale/distribution in their imported form. "Every article of foreign origin," or, in specified circumstances, its container, "shall be marked in a conspicuous place as legibly, indelibly, and permanently as the nature of the article (or container) will permit in such manner as to indicate to the ultimate purchaser in the United States the English name of the country of origin of the article."[15] An imported article's "country of origin" is the country or place where it last underwent "substantial transformation."[16] Substantial transformation is a manufacturing or other process that results in a new and different article of commerce, having a new name, character, and use that is different from that which existed prior to the processing.

E.g., Third party labeled chemicals imported from Germany in commercial packaging for resale would be labeled as "Made in Germany."

Importation of Foreign Articles for Repackaging in the United States:

The Tariff Act also regulates foreign-origin articles that are imported into the United States for further repackaging or manipulation prior to sale/distribution. Articles intended to be repacked in retail containers shall be marked, at the time of importation and following repackaging, to indicate the country of origin of the article in accordance with Country of Origin Marking requirements of the United States Customs Service, Department of Treasury (see 19 C.F.R. 134.11 above). The importer must certify to Customs, in writing at the time of importation that after repackaging the products will be re-labeled with the country of origin.

E.g., Bulk chemicals imported from Germany and repacked in the US into commercial packaging for resale would be labeled as "Made in Germany."

Importation of Foreign Articles for Further Processing/ Manufacture in the United States:

Importation of foreign-origin components that will undergo substantial transformation in the US are regulated by the Tariff Act. When an imported article will be substantially transformed in the United States, country of origin marking ***at the time*** of importation is not required, because the manufacturer is seen, for statutory purposes, to be the "ultimate purchaser" that creates a new article having a name, character, or use differing from that of the imported article.[17] The outermost containers, however, of the imported articles shall be marked.[18]

E.g. Bulk chemicals imported from Germany, reacted with other US chemicals to form a new compound and repacked in the US into commercial packaging for resale. Outer container of German bulk chemical must be labeled "Made in Germany." Final end product will follow FTC labeling requirements.

Manufacture of Articles in the United States of US Components:

The Tariff Act does not regulate the country of origin marking requirements for products that are manufactured in the United States of components that are of US origin.

All foreign-origin and US-origin articles sold in the United States must also follow the labeling requirements of the Federal Trade Commission. A detailed discussion of these requirements follows.

Federal Trade Commission Act

Foreign-origin articles fall under the jurisdiction of both the Tariff Act and the Foreign Trade Commission Act. As previously discussed, these articles must be marked with the name of the foreign country of origin in order to clear Customs entry at the US border. The FTC also has jurisdiction over foreign origin claims in packaging insofar as they go beyond the disclosure required by Customs (e.g., claims that supplement a required foreign origin marking, so as to represent where additional processing or finishing of a product occurred). In addition, the FTC has jurisdiction over foreign-origin claims in advertising, which Customs does not regulate. The FTC is charged with preventing deception and unfairness in the marketplace. The FTC Act gives the Commission the power to bring law enforcement actions against false or misleading claims that a product is of US origin.

Articles, which are substantially transformed or wholly manufactured in the United States, are under the exclusive jurisdiction of the FTC labeling regulations. According to the FTC, US content **must** be disclosed on automobiles and textile, wool, and fur products. There is, however, no law that requires most other products sold in the US to be marked or labeled "Made in USA" or have any other disclosure about their amount of US content. However, manufacturers and marketers who **choose** to make claims about the amount of US content in their products must comply with the FTC's "Made in USA" policy.[19]

For a product to be called "Made in USA," or claimed to be of domestic origin without qualifications or limits on the claim, the product must be "all or virtually all" made in the US. The term "United States," as referred to in the Enforcement Policy Statement, includes the 50 states, the District of Columbia, and the US territories and possessions. "All or virtually all" means that all significant parts and processing that go into the product must be of US origin. That is, the product should contain no, or negligible, foreign content.

On the other hand, a qualified "Made in USA" claim describes the extent, amount, or type of a product's domestic content or processing; it indicates that the product isn't entirely of domestic origin. Such a claim is appropriate for products that include US content or processing but don't meet the criteria for making an unqualified *Made in USA* claim.

No FTC statutes or regulations govern specific labeling requirements with regard to foreign versus US content. FTC practice is completely administrative (advisory and staff opinions). For purposes of determining if a product may be labeled "Made in the USA." or an equivalent expression, the FTC has employed the following cost analysis:

1. 100% US – If the product is 100% US parts and labor, it may be labeled as *"Made in the USA"* or any equivalent expression.

2. 100% foreign – If the product is entirely of foreign origin, it must be labeled with a foreign country of origin label pursuant to Customs jurisdiction. See above.

3. 50% or more US – If more than 50% of the value of the product (parts plus labor) is US, the manufacturer may:

1. remain completely silent about country of origin (thereby not deceiving the public); or

2. provide an accurate disclosure of foreign component parts, i.e., *"Made in the USA of American and X country component parts."* [In other words, if less than 50% of the value is foreign, it is not considered to be deceptive to remain silent, but if disclose anything, must disclose it all.] The FTC also allows qualified claims such as, *"Made in the USA of US and imported parts,"* or *"Made in the USA from German components,"* or *"60% US Content."*

4. 50% or more foreign – If more than 50% of the value of the product is foreign, the manufacturer must accurately disclose the foreign component parts *"Made in USA of American, Taiwanese and Chinese parts."*

5. 50%-50% Split – No advisory opinion has been issued regarding a 50%-50% split of US and foreign value. According to the FTC, given the nature of a complete cost breakdown (parts plus labor); it is unlikely that an exact 50%-50% split would occur.

As they say, "necessity is the mother of invention." The imposition of high tariffs on imports from China following years of normally declining tariffs was a shock to those who established supply chains in China. Overnight, they were faced with dramatically higher product costs. This necessity of their business to adjust to this unanticipated development forced them to reconsider how they might manage increases to their landed cost. The strategies set forth in this chapter were employed by many businesses but as you can see, require careful analysis and assessment of potential risks.

Case Study: Apparel and Footwear Manufacturers

Have you ever wondered why apparel companies aggressively market "moisture wicking" and other fabrics made of artificial fibers? Or that most shoes aren't made of genuine leather? The answer is simple: apparel made of artificial fibers and shoes made of alternatives to leather are subject to lower customs duties than clothing made from cotton or shoes made from genuine leather. It's not easy to find an all-cotton product from any major athletic brand, nor an all-leather shoe at a reasonable price point.

This practice of apparel and footwear companies is instructive for any the commercialization of ***any*** imported product. In both the product design and development processes, careful attention should be paid to the opportunity to substitute alternative materials for the product that result in the product being subject to lower customs duties. This is a standard analysis employed by sophisticated manufacturers and typically involves tradeoffs between the desires of product designers and sales teams and those responsible for achieving a landed cost of the product that is aligned with consumer expectations.

It is worth noting, however, that trade arrangements with certain trade zones in Egypt or from the [Mauritius Island] allow cotton products to be imported to the US without duty. Again, no wonder many cotton products are made in the Giza area of Egypt or assembled in the Mauritius Islands.

However, purchasing cotton product from low-duty jurisdictions will not necessarily result in a lower landed cost for your product. Cotton suppliers and manufacturers who enjoy trade preferences do not operate in a vacuum. Instead, they are well-acquainted with the cost structure of their competitors in other regions that specialize in cotton products. Not surprisingly, they charge a higher first-cost for their products that typically makes their landed cost more or less the same as that for cotton products produced in countries subject to high tariffs.

| 10 |

COVID-19

"Initial pandemic-era expectations for a double-digit decline in world merchandise trade in 2020 did not materialize. The volume of global trade has recovered to the pre-pandemic level at an extraordinarily fast pace from around mid-2020." -OECD study

Global trade has proved resilient during the COVID-19 pandemic. After a brief dip in early 2020, worldwide imports and exports recovered to pre-pandemic levels by late in the year and grew strongly in 2021. The World Trade Organization (WTO) expects trade to continue to grow by double-digit margins throughout 2022. In a recently issued report, the WTO concluded that it would be unlikely for the pandemic to have long-term implications on the role exports and imports play in the global economy. In other words, smart businesses must continue to engage in the growing global economy.

The challenges of manufacturing and sourcing products offshore are still in a state of unrest during this time of global recovery. Importers must navigate shipping delays, increased shipping costs, port congestion, labor shortages, and power disruptions—all related in some way to the fallout from the pandemic. This makes one fondly remember the days when the leading disruption to international trade were tariffs!

The challenges faced by businesses seeking to implement efficient and resilient supply chains require experience and expert management.

How to Manage COVID-19-Related Supply Chain Disruptions

The good news is that in many ways, the economy is looking bright. And there has been a shift from the consumption of services to the consumption of products. Consumers are shopping more than ever and the high demand for all kinds of products is keeping supplier manufacturers around the globe in business and on their toes. Businesses are also under tremendous pressure to keep their supply chains functioning smoothly. By now, even the average consumer is aware of the ongoing pandemic-related shipping delays and increased ocean rates because they are experiencing it firsthand. The rising cost of day-to-day products and delivery delays has trickled down to everyday life.

In short, getting back to business after the pandemic is a perfect catch-22. The demand for products is high, but suppliers are lacking inventory and/or experiencing substantial delays that began with factory worker shortages, transportation issues relating to a lack of shipping containers, available space, dockworker shortages, unloading delays, and port congestion. The list goes on! The residual business effects of the COVID-19 pandemic do not seem to be going away anytime soon. Most observers expect this trend to continue through the end of 2021 as demand for imported goods continues to be going strong, especially for the holiday season.

The COVID-19 pandemic has underscored the need of businesses to diligently work to navigate these challenges by exploring all options to ensure goods are shipped and delivered in the most efficient and cost-effective way, including:

- Adjust inventory planning by placing orders early with consideration of longer shipping lead time
- Book shipping as early as possible to secure space
- Explore alternative ports to ship or receive goods depending on the gravity of port congestion

- Be flexible with inland shipping routes and methods

Despite your best efforts to manage your supply chain, the COVID-19 pandemic has been disruptive. Most businesses have been forced to accept higher costs and pass them along to their customers.

An Alternative to Consider: Nearshoring

Due to all the global challenges that we are facing around the world, nearshoring is becoming an increasingly attractive alternative. Nearshoring isn't easy but can involve multiple benefits:

- Lower customs and duty charges
- Closer proximity allows for more frequent visits to factories/manufacturing site
- Improved control over intellectual property
- Improved language barrier and similar time zones for clearer and effective communication
- Quicker transit from manufacturing site to client
- Better speed to market
- Better control on supply chain
- Generally, more oversight and control of process for higher quality product

Post Pandemic Resiliency

It has been over two years since the outbreak of COVID-19. During this time, many companies have faced unforeseen obstacles and some of them were even forced to close their door. Despite all the challenges, there are some companies that have grown to see the pandemic as an opportunity to improve their supply chain strategy.

The pandemic was a "wake-up call" for many companies. It required businesses to rethink supply chain strategy, formulate plans for future disruptions, and learn a valuable lesson—cost is not the only consideration.

Many manufacturers across numerous industries still rely on a single source for the supply of materials and components. By multi-sourcing materials and components, companies tend to better mitigate potential delays and interruptions.

What is multi-sourcing? How to have a resilient supply chain?

As described above, a key strategy to managing supply chain risk is to create both efficient and resilient supply chains. One of the ways to achieve this is to multi-source. By obtaining raw materials, components, and services from many suppliers as opposed to a single supplier, you are better prepared and have alternate options if there is a problem. Being efficient and resilient involves increased transparency throughout the supply chain. Multi-sourcing products to reduce dependence on one supplier, diversification of the supply chain among multiple geographies, and developing long-term relationships give your clients' suppliers the confidence to become inventory partners.

For many businesses, initiatives to enhance supply chain resiliency began in response to China trade tensions but have accelerated during COVID-19 pandemic. Many already had resilient supply chains established prior to the pandemic. The future of supply chains perhaps will be more focused on resilience and stability than cost. And they will likely move closer to where their customers are located (i.e. away from China). Supply chains will be more communicative, more transparent, and for some of the companies there will possibly be more suppliers than before. In any case, future supply chains will very likely look quite different than they do today.

| 11 |

HOW DO I MAKE MY SUPPLY CHAIN TAX EFFICIENT?

"In this world nothing is certain except death and taxes."
—Benjamin Franklin

Over the years, I've observed a common trend of businesses that outsource the production of their product: by rationalizing their product cost to world markets, the business becomes more profitable and new markets become available to it; as the business grows globally, the business owners wonder why they must pay US taxes on a product *made and sold* overseas. This is a great question and reflects the fact that the United States tax system is in many respects anti-competitive by world-wide standards.

In response to our uncompetitive tax system, many US businesses have developed elaborate strategies to defer United States taxes on their foreign earnings. For example, Apple is well-known for its "Double Irish with a Dutch Sandwich," which allowed it more profits around the world, deferring US taxes, relying by transferring intellectual property licensing royalties to the low tax jurisdiction of Ireland. Likewise, one of the largest trading partners of China is the British Virgin Islands, an island inhabited by only 30,000 people! Yet, as a zero-tax offshore jurisdiction favored by trading company affiliates of US and European companies, huge volumes of business has flowed through British Virgin Island companies. While there has been criticism (often legitimate) of elaborate tax-deferral structures, it should be noted that their root lies in the US tax system itself, which taxes US companies on their global income, unlike most Western countries, which tax income on a territorial basis at its source. For example, a British company that manufactures a product in China and sells it to a customer in Germany pays no UK tax whatsoever, since its income is sourced outside the UK.

Much of the United States tax code affecting international business was established 60 years ago. Then only the top hundred or so United States companies conducted international business, the likes of General Electric, IBM, and large energy companies. Subpart F of the internal code was enacted to prevent these companies from shifting US income offshore.

Since the adoption of Subpart F under the Kennedy Administration, however, the pace of globalization has exploded. Now virtually all the American businesses—not just the Fortune 500—exist in a highly competitive global economy. As a result, competitive pressure created incentives for small businesses to structure their international operations in a manner that is more operationally and tax efficient. Common tax deferral strategies involve transferring of a business important intellectual property offshore and the formation of offshore trading companies to buy and resell sourced products to their customers. If properly structured, these business organizations can result in substantial United State tax deferrals and, in turn, provide a source of growth capital for your business.

Throughout the years, I've worked with many companies to develop and implement operationally and tax-efficient international business structures. These structures must be entered into carefully based on consultation with your legal and tax advisors.

Case Study: Automotive Components Distributor

In 2008 we were hired by a distributor of automotive components. It desired to source certain automotive components directly from low-cost suppliers in Asia. By buying directly from a low-cost supplier, it obviously had the opportunity to realize larger profit margins on the sales of its products.

Once we established an efficient supply chain for these products, we approached the client to suggest a revised business model under which most of the profit from product sourced from factories in Asia and sold directly to its customers in full container loads could be subject to deferred US taxation. The US tax deferral opportunity was substantial.

With the client's approval, we recommended adjustments to its business structure that resulted in both operational and tax efficiencies. By deferring US taxation and accumulating cash offshore, the client dramatically reduced use of its bank line of credit to support inventory purchases, thereby reducing its interest expense. By reducing its tax and operational costs, it became dramatically more profitable.

Note: While tax deferral opportunities can be substantial, they should only be considered after seeking competent legal counsel and careful analysis by your CPA.

| 12 |

CAN I DO IT MYSELF?

"An expert is someone who knows some of the worst mistakes that can be made in his subject, and how to avoid them." —Werner Heisenberg

In the introduction to this book, I stated that my purpose was to share some of what I've learned over the years about international trade and what it takes to establish an efficient and resilient supply chain. While this book explores sourcing fundamentals the standard product sourcing process and a number of other considerations, I would do you a disservice not to warn you against repeating my education in the school of hard knocks.

Many universities have specialized majors in supply chain management and their graduates staff the supply chain divisions of some of the world's best corporations. To think that you can manage your own supply chain without costly errors is, candidly, naïve.

Perhaps you *could* do it yourself, but the question is whether this is the best use of your time. How much time and money are you willing to invest? How many times are you willing to restart the process? My observation is that supply chain management is not the strength of most small businesses, nor is it their largest opportunity to increase their profitability. Companies I have had the privilege of working with over time have hired our firm Global Nexus (www.globalnxs.com) in order to allow them to focus higher value initiative, including marketing, sales, acquisition of other companies, and the like. Especially in today's world, where a sophisticated business may have a supply chain touching multiple countries, the skillset and time required to create and manage that supply chain is a large job, especially across multiple time zones, cultures, and languages.

One of the biggest challenges of creating a supply chain by yourself is the need of regular interaction with your factories, especially to conduct quality control inspections and coordinate freight logistics. The efficient performance of this work requires a team that understands business and cultural norms at your factory. This staff must also have a detailed understanding of the factoring processes utilized to make your product and unique features and quality vulnerabilities of your product. It is challenging to identify, recruit, and manage an in-country staff and language barriers may come at time differences and different cultural norms. For most businesses, it is much more efficient to hire third-party contractors to provide these services.

The need for competent local staff is even more critical if a quality product problem arises with your product or if your supply chain is interrupted by unforeseen events (e.g., COVID-19, port closures). In these circumstances, it is invaluable to have "boots-on-the-ground" that can interact with your factory and other links in your supply chain to efficiently resolve issues.

Another reason to outsource management of your supply chain involves your ability to leverage their expertise. As noted above, supply chain management is a sophisticated academic discipline. Those who understand it will help your business save time and money at levels well beyond the cost of such services. Perhaps most importantly, your utilization of third-party experts will allow you to focus on opportunities to make your business more profitable that are better aligned with your own unique skillset.

Another factor making it challenging to manage your supply chain from your home office involves the necessity of face-to-face interaction. As COVID-19 has taught us, we shouldn't assume that international travel will be easy, or even allowed. As shared in this book, building trust is perhaps the most critical factor to successfully managing your supply chain. Most business executives simply can't take time out of their schedules to be face-to-face with their suppliers in foreign land.

These are a few of the reasons we would suggest that you go it alone. On the other hand, as communicated in this book, sourcing products is not rocket science. With the devotion of enough time and resources and willingness to absorb the cost and delays of inevitable mistakes, eventually you may be successful in establishing a supply chain. And if you don't, know that you can shout to us at any time. Some of our best customers are those who initially tried to set up a supply chain on their own.

| 13 |

NEXT STEPS WITH GLOBAL NEXUS

Now that you have absorbed all the information in this book, what can you do next?

Using the information you have learned from this book, how can you now move forward with confidence in terms of manufacturing overseas?

And how can you do it in a way that helps you produce the best product and also have a smooth experience that won't divert focus from other business goals or lead to major risk?

The answer is simple . . .

If you want to manufacture overseas, it's wise to work with industry experts who can provide you with the inside knowledge and information you need to streamline your manufacturing process and minimize the associated risk.

As you learned throughout this book, the benefits of sourcing and manufacturing products overseas are plentiful, but the process is extremely complex.

There is no doubt that you need an industry expert to help you find the right factory, ensure the success of your product, find the best shipping company, and all the in between. There are simply too many moving parts to offshore manufacturing, and proceeding with an expert is vital to your success. Your business depends on you to make the right decision and do things the right way the first time around . . .

We are the industry experts who are available to help you on your manufacturing and product sourcing journey!

If you are already manufacturing and need a supply chain audit on your existing process, or if you are currently manufacturing domestically and want guidance on outsourcing overseas, we're confident that we can help improve your supply chain efficiency while enhancing transparency and mitigating key risks.

Our goal is to provide the clarity and guidance you need to make a winning move.

This is why we are offering you a complementary product sourcing consultation to better understand your company and product outsourcing needs.

To claim your complimentary consultation, please visit http://go.globalnxs.com/consultation.

We look forward to helping you and your company succeed in sourcing and manufacturing products overseas.

John C. Ramig

President and Founder

Global Nexus Manufacturing and Sourcing Solutions

https://www.globalnxs.com/

tel: 503.546.3480

GLOSSARY OF TERMS

Manufacturing Outsourcing. As used in this book, the term manufacturing outsourcing refers to practice by a business of outsourcing to a third-party factory for the manufacturer of its unique product. This typically involves the business providing its outsourcing factory with product and packaging specifications that bear the IP trademark or other unique branding information. For example, Nike outsources the manufacture of its footwear and apparel products. These products are manufactured with one or more Nike trademarks and utilize other intellectual property and unique product designs that are licensed to the factory.

Sourcing. As used in this book, sourcing refers to the purchase of a product for business *already being made* by a third-party factory. For example, a healthcare system may use nitrile gloves that meet generic, industry specifications from one or more suppliers.

Silk Road. The Silk Road was a series of ancient trade networks to connect to China and the Far East with countries in Europe and the Middle East. The "Road" included a group of trading posts and markets that were used to help in the storage, transport, and exchange of goods. The Silk Road was important because it helped to generate trade and commerce between a number of different kingdoms and empires. This helped for ideas, culture, invention, and unique products to spread across much of the settled world.

Spice Route. The Spice Routes, also known as Maritime Silk Roads, is the name given to the network of sea routes that link the East and the West. They stretch from the west coast of Japan through the islands of Indonesia, around India to the lands of the Middle East, and from there across the Mediterranean to Europe.

Suez Canal. The Suez Canal is an artificial sea-level waterway in Egypt, connecting the Mediterranean Sea to the Red Sea through the Isthmus Suez and dividing Africa and Asia. The canals are a route of trade between Europe and Asia.

Mercantilism. Mercantilism is a system "of trade that spanned from the 16th century to the 18th century" in which a country attempts to amass wealth through trade with other countries, exporting more than it imports and increasing source of gold and precious metals.

General Agreement on Tariffs and Trade (GATT). The General Agreement on Tariffs and Trade, signed on October 30, 1947, by 23 countries, was a legal agreement minimizing barriers to international trade by eliminating or reducing quotas, tariffs, and subsidies while preserving significant regulations. The objectives of GATT (i) helped raised standards of living; (ii) achieve full employment; (iii) develop the world's resources; (iv) expand production and the exchange of goods; and (v) promote economic development. GATT was refined over the years and ultimately replaced by the World Trade Organization on January 1, 1995.

Freight Forwarder. A freight forwarder is a person or company that organizes shipments for individual corporations to get goods from the manufacturer producer to a market, customer or final point of distribution. Freight forwarders contact with a carrier or often multiple carriers to move goods from one country to another. A freight forwarder does move the goods but acts as an expert in the logistics network. A freight forwarder typically utilizes a variety of shipping modes including ships, airplanes, trucks, and railroads and often uses multiple modes for a single shipment.

FDA Certification. FDA stands for the Food and Drug Administration, a United States government agency responsible for the safety of food, dietary supplements, human drugs, vaccines, blood products and other biologicals, medical devices, radiation-emitting electronics, cosmetics, veterinarian products, and tobacco products being sold or manufactured in the United States. The FDA also inspects and enforces regulations related to those industries. Organizations that manufacture, repack, or reliable products in these industries generally register with the FDA.

First Cost. The cost of a product directly from the factory source. This price is after FOB a shipping port proximate to the factory.

Landed Cost. The cost of "landing" a product in your distribution center, which typically includes the first cost of the product, shipping insurance, and any applicable customs duties.

ISO (International Organization for Standardization). ISO is an independent, nongovernmental international organization that develops standards to ensure the quality, safety and efficiency of products, services, and systems. An ISO certified factory generally can be relied upon to have in place basic manufacturing processes.

Box Maker Certificate. A box maker certificate is a seal printed on the bottom of a box that tells you how strong it is. It is not legally required, but it's proof that the box has been properly tested and rated.

UL Certification. Underwriter Laboratories (UL) is one of the oldest safety certification companies in existence. They certify products, facilities, processes, or systems based on industry-wide standards. By doing so, they issue over 20 different certifications in a wide range of categories. UL listings has tested representative samples of a product and determined that the product meets specific, defined requirements. These requirements are often based on UL and nationally recognized standards for safety.

Tariff. Tariff is a tax or duty imposed on a particular class of goods and services imported from another country. Governments impose tariffs to raise revenue, protect domestic industries, or exert political leverage over another country. Tariffs often result in unwanted side effects such as higher consumer prices. Tariffs have a long and contentious history in the debate over whether they represent good or bad policy rages on to this day.

Tooling. Tooling refers to the factoring components machines needed for production. Common categories of machine tooling include fixtures, gauges, molds, dyes, cutting equipment and patterns. 3D is the action or process of making a physical object from a digital file. The creation of a 3D object is achieved using additive processes. In an additive process, an object is created by laying down successive layers of material until the object is created. Using 3D printing to create prototypes expedites the product development process.

ENDNOTES

1.   ˆ This chapter borrows extensively from the following articles on global trade: Vanham, Peter. "A brief history of globalization." World Economic Forum. 17 Jan, 2019; Economic Report to the President, Government Pending Office, [date].

2.   ˆ These products are subject to the labeling requirements of the American Automobile Labeling Act, Textile Fiber Products Identification Act, the Wool Products Labeling Act, or the Fur Products Labeling Act.

3.   ˆ The policy statement is available at https://www.ftc.gov/public-statements/1997/12/enforcement-policy-statement-us-origin-claims (the "Policy Statement").

4.   ˆ The FTC discusses these factors in detail in the Policy Statement.

5.   ˆ *See* the Policy Statement.

6.   ˆ 19 CFR § 134.35(a).

7.   ˆ *Cummins Engine Co. v. United States*, 23 C.I.T. 1019, 1034–35 (1999) (quoting *Gibson-Thomsen Co.* Quotations omitted).

8.   ˆ https://www.ftc.gov/public-statements/1997/12/enforcement-policy-statement-us-origin-claims.

9.   ˆ *US v. Gibson-Thomsen Co.*, 1 ITRD 1176 (C.C.P.A. 1940).

10.   ˆ 19 CFR § 134.35(a).

11.   ˆ 48 CFR § 25.101(a).

12.   ˆ 48 CFR § 25.003.

13.   ˆ Federal Trade Commission Act, 15 USC. § 45.

14.   ˆ Tariff Act, 19 USC. § 1304.

15.   ˆ 19 C.F.R. 134.11, 19 USC.A § 1304(a). See also, Lanham Act § 42 (providing that no imported goods bearing a name or mark calculated to induce the public to believe that a foreign article is manufactured in the United States or that it is manufactured in any foreign country or locality other than the true country or locality shall be admitted to entry into the United States).

16.   ˆ Target Sportswear, Inc. v. US, 19 Ct. Int'l Trade 65, 875 F. Supp. 835, 17 Int'l Trade Re. (BNA) 1043 (1995), decision aff'd, 70 F.3d 604, 17 Int'l Trade

Re. (BNA) 2025 (Fed. Cir. 1995), cert. denied, 517 US 1208, 116 S. Ct. 1824, 134 L. Ed. 2d 929, 18 Int'l Trade Re. (BNA) 1352 (1996).

17.   ˆ 19 CFR 134.35(a). See also, US v. Gibson-Thomsen Co., Inc., 27 C.C.P.A. 267, C.A.D. 98, Int'l Trade Re. (BNA) 1176, 1940 WL 4085 (1940).

18.   ˆ 19 CFR 134.35(a).

19.   ˆ See http://www.ftc.gov/os/statutes/usajump.htm.

John C. Ramig is the founder and president of Global Nexus, a worldwide leader in manufacturing & sourcing solutions. Global Nexus exists to help small and medium-sized businesses reap the numerous benefits of outsourcing while managing its complexities and risks with the help of our dedicated, expert staff. You can connect with John and his team at https://www.globalnxs.com.